T0167493

Resetting Our Future

A Global Playbook
for the Next Pandemic

RESETTING OUR FUTURE

A Global Playbook for the Next Pandemic

Anne Kabagambe

CHANGEMAKERS
BOOKS

Winchester, UK
Washington, USA

JOHN HUNT PUBLISHING

First published by Changemakers Books, 2021
Changemakers Books is an imprint of John Hunt Publishing Ltd., No. 3 East Street,
Alresford, Hampshire SO24 9EE, UK
office@jhpbooks.com
www.johnhuntpublishing.com
www.changemakers-books.com

For distributor details and how to order please visit the 'Ordering' section on our website.

Text copyright: Anne Kabagambe 2020

ISBN: 978 1 78904 759 2
978 1 78904 760 8 (ebook)
Library of Congress Control Number: 2020945894

A CIP catalogue record for this book is available from the British Library.

Design: Stuart Davies

Printed and bound by CPI Group (UK) Ltd, Croydon, CR0 4YY
Printed in North America by CPI GPS partners

We operate a distinctive and ethical publishing philosophy in
all areas of our business, from our global network of authors to
production and worldwide distribution.

Contents

The *Resetting Our Future* Series

At this critical moment of history, with a pandemic raging, we have the rare opportunity for a Great Reset – to choose a different future. This series provides a platform for pragmatic thought leaders to share their vision for change based on their deep expertise. For communities and nations struggling to cope with the crisis, these books will provide a burst of hope and energy to help us take the first difficult steps towards a better future.

– Tim Ward, publisher, Changemakers Books

What if Solving the Climate Crisis Is Simple?
Tom Bowman, President of Bowman Change, Inc., and Writing Team Lead for the U.S. ACE National Strategic Planning Framework

Zero Waste Living, the 80/20 Way
The Busy Person's Guide to a Lighter Footprint
Stephanie Miller, Founder of Zero Waste in DC, and former Director, IFC Climate Business Department.

A Chicken Can't Lay a Duck Egg
How COVID-19 can Solve the Climate Crisis
Graeme Maxton, (former Secretary-General of the Club of Rome), and Bernice Maxton-Lee (former Director, Jane Goodall Institute)

A Global Playbook for the Next Pandemic
Anne Kabagambe, World Bank Executive Director

We Should have Seen it Coming
How Foresight can Prepare us for the Next Crisis
Bart Édes, North American Representative, Asian Development Bank

Impact ED
A Roadmap for Restoring Jobs & Rebuilding the Economy
Rebecca Corbin (President, National Association of
Community College Entrepreneurship), Andrew Gold
and Mary-Beth Kerly (both business faculty, Hillsborough
Community College).

Power Switch
How Activists can win the Fight Against Extreme Inequality
Paul O'Brien, VP, Policy and Advocacy, Oxfam America

Creating a Paradigm Shift to Achieve the Global SDGs
A SMART Futures Mindset for a Sustainable World.
Dr. Claire Nelson, Chief Visionary Officer and Lead Futurist,
The Futures Forum

Reconstructing Blackness
Rev. Charles Howard, Chaplin, University of
Pennsylvania, Philadelphia.

Cut Super Climate Pollutants, Now!
The Ozone Treaty's Urgent Lessons for Speeding up Climate Action
Alan Miller (former World Bank representative for global
climate negotiations) and Durwood Zaelke, (President, The
Institute for Governance & Sustainable Development, and
co-director, The Program on Governance for Sustainable
Development at UC Santa Barbara)

www.ResettingOurFuture.com

To the millions of global citizens living under the poverty line, to whom this book is dedicated. Here is to the hope of building a better and more inclusive post-pandemic world.

Preface and Disclaimer

This book originated from an op-ed I penned for the Milken Institute back in June 2020. This was at a time when the world was in the process of re-opening after three months of global lockdown. The rallying cry then was how to open the economy without sowing the seeds for an even more devastating return of COVID-19. At that time I was serving as Executive Director on the Board of the World Bank Group, focused daily on issues of saving lives and livelihood. This caused me to reflect on the singular urgency of a globally coordinated response to pandemics, and how the current development architecture contains the building blocks required for the system to work. How we might put those blocks together is the subject of this book.

This book does not in any form or shape reflect the views of the World Bank Group, nor represent the opinion of its management team. I wish, however, to pay tribute to colleagues both inside and outside the institution who were instrumental in shaping my thoughts on a global playbook for the next pandemic – and most importantly, to the billions of global citizens still living under the poverty line, to whom this book is dedicated.

Foreword

by Thomas Lovejoy

The Pandemic has changed our world. Lives have been lost. Livelihoods as well. Far too many face urgent problems of health and economic security, but almost all of us are reinventing our lives in one way or another. Meeting the immediate needs of the less fortunate is obviously a priority, and a big one. But beyond those compassionate imperatives, there is also tremendous opportunity for what some people are calling a "Great Reset." This series of books, *Resetting Our Future*, is designed to provide pragmatic visionary ideas and stimulate a fundamental rethink of the future of humanity, nature and the economy.

I find myself thinking about my parents, who had lived through the Second World War and the Great Depression, and am still impressed by the sense of frugality they had attained. When packages arrived in the mail, my father would save the paper and string; he did it so systematically I don't recall our ever having to buy string. Our diets were more careful: whether it could be afforded or not, beef was restricted to once a week. When aluminum foil – the great boon to the kitchen – appeared, we used and washed it repeatedly until it fell apart. Bottles, whether coca cola or milk, were recycled.

Waste was consciously avoided. My childhood task was to put out the trash; what goes out of my backdoor today is an unnecessary multiple of that. At least some of it now goes to recycling but a lot more should surely be possible.

There was also a widespread sense of service to a larger community. Military service was required of all. But there was also the Civilian Conservation Corps, which had provided jobs and repaired the ecological destruction that had generated the Dust Bowl. The Kennedy administration introduced the Peace

Corps and the President's phrase "Ask not what your country can do for you but what you can do for your country" still resonates in our minds.

There had been antecedents, but in the 1970s there was a global awakening about a growing environmental crisis. In 1972, The United Nations held its first conference on the environment at Stockholm. Most of the modern US institutions and laws about environment were established under moderate Republican administrations (Nixon and Ford). Environment was seen not just as appealing to "greenies" but also as a thoughtful conservative's issue. The largest meeting of Heads of State in history, the Earth Summit, took place in Rio de Janeiro in 1992 and three international conventions – climate change, biodiversity (on which I was consulted) and desertification – came into existence.

But three things changed. First, there now are three times as many people alive today as when I was born and each new person deserves a minimum quality of life. Second, the sense of frugality was succeeded by a growing appetite for affluence and an overall attitude of entitlement. And third, conservative political advisors found advantage in demonizing the environment as comity vanished from the political dialogue.

Insufficient progress has brought humanity and the environment to a crisis state. The CO2 level in the atmosphere at 415 ppm (parts per million) is way beyond a non-disruptive level around 350 ppm. (The pre-industrial level was 280 ppm.)

Human impacts on nature and biodiversity are not just confined to climate change. Those impacts will not produce just a long slide of continuous degradation. The Pandemic is a direct result of intrusion upon, and destruction of, nature as well as wild-animal trade and markets. The scientific body of the UN Convention on Biological Diversity warned in 2020 that we could lose a million species unless there are major changes in human interactions with nature.

We still can turn those situations around. Ecosystem restoration at scale could pull carbon back out of the atmosphere for a soft landing at 1.5 degrees of warming (at 350 ppm), hand in hand with a rapid halt in production and use of fossil fuels. The Amazon tipping point where its hydrological cycle would fail to provide enough rain to maintain the forest in southern and eastern Amazonia can be solved with major reforestation. The oceans' biology is struggling with increasing acidity, warming and ubiquitous pollution with plastics: addressing climate change can lower the first two and efforts to remove plastics from our waste stream can improve the latter.

Indisputably, we need a major reset in our economies, what we produce, and what we consume. We exist on an amazing living planet, with a biological profusion that can provide humanity a cornucopia of benefits – and more that science has yet to reveal – and all of it is automatically recyclable because nature is very good at that. Scientists have determined that we can, in fact, feed all the people on the planet, and the couple billion more who may come, by a combination of selective improvements of productivity, eliminating food waste and altering our diets (which our doctors have been advising us to do anyway).

The *Resetting Our Future* series is intended to help people think about various ways of economic and social rebuilding that will support humanity for the long term. There is no single way to do this and there is plenty of room for creativity in the process, but nature with its capacity for recovery and for recycling can provide us with much inspiration, including ways beyond our current ability to imagine.

Ecosystems do recover from shocks, but the bigger the shock, the more complicated recovery can be. At the end of the Cretaceous period (66 million years ago) a gigantic meteor slammed into the Caribbean near the Yucatan and threw up so much dust and debris into the atmosphere that much of biodiversity perished. It was *sayonara* for the dinosaurs; their only surviving close relatives were precursors to modern day birds. It certainly was not a good time for life on Earth.

The clear lesson of the pandemic is that it makes no sense to generate a global crisis and then hope for a miracle. We are lucky to have the pandemic help us reset our relation to the Living Planet as a whole. We already have building blocks like the United Nations Sustainable Development Goals and various environmental Conventions to help us think through more effective goals and targets. The imperative is to rebuild with humility and imagination, while always conscious of the health of the living planet on which we have the joy and privilege to exist.

Dr. Thomas E. Lovejoy is Professor of Environmental Science and Policy at George Mason University and a Senior Fellow at the United Nations Foundation. A world-renowned conservation biologist, Dr. Lovejoy introduced the term "biological diversity" to the scientific community.

Chapter 1

Global Pandemics – Emerging Realities

A Brief History of Pandemics

Throughout history humankind has grappled with the existential threat of catastrophic pandemics. The Great Influenza of 1918–1920 (Spanish Flu) was the deadliest in the past century, killing more people than those who died in the whole of World War I. Pandemics are defined by the World Health Organization as an epidemic occurring worldwide, or over a very wide area, crossing international boundaries and usually affecting a large number of people. In the past, such outbreaks have devastated societies, determined the outcomes of wars, killed a sizable percentage of populations, and destroyed entire economies. Ironically, pandemics had silver linings in their aftermath: they fostered innovations and advances in sciences, economics, and political systems. While there have been a hundred years between the Great Influenza pandemic and the COVID-19 pandemic, historical epidemiology indicates that humankind has constantly been under threat of smaller pandemics not at the scale of the deadly Spanish Flu or the current novel coronavirus that gave us the disease named COVID-19. Each one of them uniquely shaped our history and society. This chapter presents a brief account of major pandemic outbreaks that have impacted the global community starting with the Great Influenza and ending with COVID-19. Knowing our history can help our global community respond with the necessary science, policy, and economics that create solutions, innovate, and care for our global population and safeguard human life. In other words, from these pandemics we can begin to glean the information we need to create a Global Pandemic Playbook from which we can address future threats and crises with the right knowledge, innovation, policy, and resources.

The Great Influenza of 1918–1920 (Spanish Flu Pandemic)

The Spanish Flu pandemic of the twentieth century was the last true global pandemic in the pre-antibiotic era in which no treatment of secondary bacterial infections was available. The secondary infections caused severe pneumonia, which was likely responsible for most of the deaths in 1918. This pandemic was caused by the H1N1 strain of the influenza virus, which had repeated outbreaks in the early years of the twenty-first century. According to the Centers for Disease Control, outbreaks of flu-like illness were first detected in the United States in March of 1918, signaling what was the beginning of the 1918 pandemic flu, also referred to as the Spanish Flu. It is suggested that it originated in the state of Kansas and then spread to Europe and Asia, but these are just theories. The failure to identify origination of the Spanish Flu is partly attributed to the fact that it happened in the middle of World War I, when a high-level censorship was commonplace, and modes of transportation were relatively advanced to facilitate intercontinental travel.[1]

The deadly influenza virus spread exponentially to every corner of the world in a span of a few months. Its massive spread to Europe was partly due to military movements and overcrowding, while its devastation in the USA, Asia, Africa, and the Pacific Islands was also pronounced. The mortality rate of Spanish Flu ranged between ten and twenty percent, claiming between 50 million and 100 million lives worldwide, including 675,000 in the United States. At its peak, over a quarter of the global population contracted flu. Unexpectedly, the H1N1 virus affected mostly young and previously healthy individuals. Its death toll in a year was more than what Black Death had killed in a century.[2]

Despite its immense effect on the global civilization and devastating impact, the Spanish Flu started to fade quickly from both public and scientific awareness, establishing a precedent for the future pandemics, and leading some historians to call it the "forgotten pandemic."[3] There are three possible explanations for this treatment of the pandemic. First, the pandemic peaked and waned rapidly over a period of 9 months before it got adequate media coverage. Second, the pandemic was overshadowed by more significant historical events, such as the culmination and the ending of World War I. Lastly, this is how societies deal with such rapidly spreading pandemics – at first with great interest, horror, and panic, and then, as soon as they start to subside, with dispassionate disinterest.

From this pandemic, which was a turning point in global public health and spurred the creation of public health systems across the developed world, we learned several scientific and policy lessons that can inform our future plans. The Spanish Flu highlighted that co-morbidity can often be the killer and not the virus itself. Thus, it brought about the science that allows us to identify early biomarkers for impending bacterial pneumonia in influenza patients so that they can be treated more rapidly. It also put into place biomedical interventions and social distancing measure for use when a pandemic strikes. These include the now-familiar strategies of closing bars, restaurants, schools, places of worship and other public gatherings and isolating or quarantining the sick.

Smallpox Outbreak in Former Yugoslavia (1972)

Smallpox was a highly contagious disease caused by the Variola virus, with prominent skin eruptions and mortality of about 30 percent. It may have been responsible for hundreds of millions of fatalities in the twentieth century alone. Due to the well-coordinated global effort starting in 1967, under the leadership of Donald Henderson, smallpox was eradicated globally within a decade.[4]

The smallpox outbreak in the former Yugoslavia in 1972 was a far cry even from an epidemic, let alone a pandemic. However, it illustrated the challenges associated with a rapidly spreading, highly contagious illness in a modern world. It started with a pilgrim returning from the Middle East, who developed fever and skin eruptions. About 10,000 individuals who may have come into contact with those infected were placed in quarantine. Borders were closed, and all non-essential travel was suspended. Within two weeks, the entire population of Yugoslavia, about 18 million people at the time, were revaccinated. During the outbreak, 175 cases were identified, with 35 fatalities. Due to prompt and massive response, however, the disease was eradicated, and the society returned to normal within two months. This event has proven to be a useful model for responses to an outbreak of a highly contagious disease, both as a natural occurrence and as an act of bioterrorism.

From the fight to eradicate smallpox we learned that large scale worldwide vaccination programs are possible and work very well to limit, and eventually end, the spread of a virus. However, it is critical to have national stockpiles of vaccines in each country's arsenal. It is also important to look closely at how long to continue mandatory vaccination campaigns to assure the real end to the disease. Surveillance and feedback reports and rapid response to outbreaks needs to exist inside individual countries and across the globe. Eradicating this pandemic succeeded in part because of successfully educating local officials across the globe and reinforcing the knowledge of authority figures such as village chiefs and elders about disease-prevention methods as well as the need for early identification and treatment. These strategies have brought an end to Smallpox and the global solidarity we created in the face of Smallpox can work for other pandemic diseases as well.

HIV Pandemic

HIV/AIDS started in the early 1980s in the USA, causing significant public concern as HIV at the time inevitably progressed to AIDS and, ultimately, to death. The initial expansion of HIV was marked by its spread predominantly among the gay population and by high mortality, leading to marked social isolation and stigma. The public health response to HIV/AIDS was slowed by this social stigma. HIV has killed about 40 million people since 1981 and currently affects about 40 million people globally.[5] It causes about one million deaths a year worldwide (down from nearly two million in 2005). While it represents a global public health phenomenon, the HIV epidemic is particularly alarming in some Sub-Saharan African countries (Botswana, Lesotho, and Swaziland), where the prevalence tops 25%.[6] In the USA, about 1.2 million people live with HIV and about 12,000 die every year (down from over 40,000 per year in the late 1990s).[7] HIV in the USA disproportionately affects the gay population, transgender women, and African Americans.

Being a fairly slow-spreading pandemic, HIV has received formidable public health attention, both by national and by international administrations and pharmaceutical companies. Thanks to the advancement in treatment, HIV has been turned into a chronic condition that can be managed by medications.

Health is a continuous process, not a destination, as proven by the millions of people living with HIV, in what is now the fourth decade of that pandemic. By remaining on guard and vigilant, individuals, countries and the global public health system eventually slowed the growth of this disease, until it plateaued. We are stronger and more effective when we take on that vigilance together. This includes early and continuous attention to social, economic and environmental circumstances that give the disease a foothold. In the fight against HIV/ AIDS individual communities developed response strategies that spoke to their people allowing education to be specific and targeted. Gender inequalities, gender-based violence and the criminalization and marginalization of vulnerable groups increase the risk of infection and policy measures are needed to create social changes to address these vulnerabilities. We also learned that when companies are allowed to hold and use intellectual property rights to their technologies for fighting disease, people die; therefore technologies and treatments need to be made available through some other means.

Severe Acute Respiratory Syndrome (SARS)

Severe Acute Respiratory Syndrome (SARS), caused by the SARS Coronavirus (SARS-CoV), was declared to be a global threat in March 2003, after first appearing in Southern China in November 2002.[8] SARS infected fewer than 10,000 individuals and left 774 people dead,[9] mainly in China and Hong Kong. It was the first severe and readily transmissible new disease to emerge in the twenty-first century and showed a clear capacity to spread along the routes of international air travel.[10] The severity of respiratory symptoms caused a global public health concern. Also, the mortality rate which was estimated to range from zero to more than fifty percent depending on the age group affected, with an overall estimate of approximately fifteen percent, was of concern.[11]

Due to the vigilance of public health systems worldwide, the outbreak was contained by mid-2003. This was possible because the World Health Organization worked closely with health authorities in affected countries to provide epidemiological, clinical, and logistical support and to bring the outbreak under control.[12] For its part, the US CDC worked closely with WHO and other partners in a global effort to address the SARS outbreak of 2003 by taking the following actions:

- Activated its Emergency Operations Center to provide round-the-clock coordination and response.
- Committed more than 800 medical experts and support staff to work on the SARS response.

- Deployed medical officers, epidemiologists, and other specialists to assist with on-site investigations around the world.

- Provided assistance to state and local health departments in investigating possible cases of SARS in the United States.

- Conducted extensive laboratory testing of clinical specimens from SARS patients to identify the cause of the disease.

- Initiated a system for distributing health alert notices to travelers who may have been exposed to cases of SARS.[13]

SARS brought an example of how to use rapid notification of health authorities and the honest reporting of cases that might cause international spread. This international collaboration is paramount both in tracking and in treatment and prevention, including scientists, public health experts, researchers, governments, nongovernmental and international organizations. They can address travel recommendations, including screening measures at airports, which appear to be effective in helping to contain the international spread of an emerging infection. These collaborators can work together to issue timely global alerts, especially when widely supported by a responsible press and amplified by electronic communications. Such alerts work well to raise awareness and vigilance to levels that can prevent imported cases of an emerging and transmissible infection from causing significant outbreaks. If the response is backed by political commitment and tailored to the circumstances, outbreaks can be contained without a curative drug or vaccine. However, weaknesses in health systems can permit emerging infections to amplify and spread and can compromise patient care. The strengthening of health systems thus deserves high priority.

"Swine Flu" or H1N1/09 Pandemic

SARS-CoV was followed by another pandemic first detected in the United States in 2009. This novel influenza virus, H1N1, colloquially referred to as Swine Flu, brought about a global influenza pandemic, so declared by the WHO on April 25, 2009. Lasting from spring 2009 to fall 2009, the H1N1 infected over ten percent of the global population and is estimated to have killed anywhere from 151,700 people to 575,400 people, according to the US CDC[14] during its first year in circulation. From April 12, 2009, to April 10, 2010, the CDC estimated that the H1N1 infected an estimated 60.8 million people, causing 274,304 hospitalizations, and killing 12,469[15] people in the United States alone. The US-led response to the H1N1 pandemic was complex and multipronged. Although its death rate was ultimately lower than the regular influenza death rates, at the time it was perceived as very threatening because it disproportionately affected previously healthy young adults, often quickly leading to severe respiratory compromise. A possible explanation for this is attributed to older adults having immunity due to a similar H1N1 outbreak in the 1970s. It culminated with the WHO's declaration that the H1N1 pandemic was over on August 10, 2010.[16]

In this case, our investments in pandemic planning and stockpiling antiviral medications paid off and we learned that adaptable and science-driven responses work when combined with clear, straightforward information provided to the public to allay fears, build trust, and change behavior. We also saw a foreshadowing of how major the ramifications are for students, parents, and employers when schools are closed and that these systems need to be addressed if pandemic disease is not going to interrupt child development as well as the economy.

The Ebola Virus Disease Outbreak (2014–2016)

The Ebola virus outbreak originated in a remote village in

Guinea in December 2013 and grew to severely impact West Africa. It spread to neighboring countries of Sierra Leone and Liberia over the following months. It infected over 28,000 people and claimed over 11,000 lives. It wrought social and economic devastation to the three most affected countries. A few cases were confirmed in Nigeria and Mali, but those outbreaks were quickly contained.

The WHO Secretariat activated an unprecedented response to the outbreak, deploying thousands of experts and medical equipment, mobilizing foreign medical teams, and coordinating the creation of mobile laboratories and treatment centers. In January 2016, WHO declared that the outbreak was finally coming to an end, and in March officially announced Ebola was no longer a public health emergency. The WHO, however, warned that flare-ups of the disease were likely to continue and that countries in the region need to remain vigilant and prepared. These developments materialized after nearly three years of unprecedented international cooperation to combat the largest Ebola outbreak in history.

Our response efforts are dependent on the ability to have rapid laboratory testing. We need that capacity along with other key capacities in place before we launch a response including leadership and coordination, technical support, logistics, management of human resources and communications. This includes national response strategies as well as international response strategies. As we saw with N1N1, school closures have enormous impacts. During the Ebola outbreak we saw increases in gender-based violence, teenage pregnancies, child marriage, exploitation, and other forms of abuse against adolescent girls (including online sexual exploitation) and so our humanitarian responses are as important as our medical responses. This includes support for survivors so that we can continue to minimize transmission. A one-size-fits-all approach to community engagement isn't effective. Each community is unique, and engagement has to be hyper-contextualized to affected communities and we must in all contexts avoid causing panic when we communicate about disease outbreaks. In the case of Ebola, we saw a rapid response funding mechanism launched by the World Health Organization so that funds were ready to jump start the response.

ZIKA (2015–2016)

Zika virus was a little known, dormant virus found in rhesus monkeys in Uganda. Before 2014, the only known outbreak among humans was recorded in Micronesia in 2007. The virus was then identified in Brazil in 2015, after an outbreak of a mild illness causing a flat pinkish rash, bloodshot eyes, fever, joint pain and headaches, resembling Dengue Fever. Zika is a mosquito-borne disease, but it can be sexually transmitted. Despite its mild course, which initially made it unremarkable from the public health perspective, infection with Zika can cause Guillain-Barre syndrome in its wake in adults and, more tragically, cause severe microcephalia in unborn children of infected mothers.

In Brazil, in 2015, for example, there were 2400 congenital disabilities and 29 infant deaths due to suspected Zika infection. Zika outbreak is an illustrative case of the context of global transmission: it was transferred from Micronesia, across the Pacific, to Brazil, whence it continued to spread. It is also a case of a modern media pandemic; it featured prominently in social media, creating awareness, but also fear and misinformation. Since 2016, Zika has continued to spread throughout South America, Central America, the Caribbean, and several states within the USA. It remains a significant public health concern, as there is no vaccine and the only reliable way to avoid the risk is to avoid areas where Zika was identified or to postpone pregnancy should travel to or living in affected areas be unavoidable.

Interestingly, Zika lessons are harder to tease out as the outbreak of this disease was compounded by a resurgence in Ebola, teaching us that we are underprepared for the kinds of multi-pronged crises that we see more and more frequently globally because of climate change. Now, the advent of COVID-19 is running into the Zika timeline also. We need to be prepared to access and analyze real time administrative data to understand vital outbreaks even in complex situations. We need to understand that communities will have different issues and need very different public health measures in complex situations, and we need to work on all aspects of healthcare simultaneously so that other factors don't undermine the work we are doing to eradicate pandemic diseases.

The Coronavirus Disease (COVID-19)

Today, the world is staring down the barrel of yet another global outbreak. Looking at the numbers, it's clear we have collectively failed at our most sacred duty, that of safeguarding human life. At the time of this writing in September 2020, the COVID-19 pandemic has claimed 15,581,009 confirmed cases and 35,173 deaths[17] globally. Six months since the start of the pandemic, the US has seen its unemployment figures soar to their highest-ever level. Across the world we have witnessed the closure of schools, of borders, the cancellation of global cultural and sporting events like the Tokyo 2020 Olympic games. Responses in the face of pandemic vary widely, from the most drastic – the lockdown of entire towns, cities, and even countries to global travel restrictions in place for most nations on earth.[18]

The COVID-19 pandemic has singularly impacted both worldwide demand and supply at the same time, setting off in its wake a financial crisis so significant that the 2008–2009 financial meltdown pales in comparison. COVID-19 has brought to bear what would be the second recession in a decade, and certainly the worst recession since World War II.[19]

This has made it necessary for leaders and policymakers not only to enact drastic public health measures, but also to pull all levers of fiscal policy available to them, and all at the same time. This includes Central Banks cutting back on interest rates to the point that they have crossed into negative territory at times. Global economic outlooks seem bleak. Economic activity among advanced economies is anticipated to shrink seven percent in 2020 as domestic demand and supply, trade, and finance have been severely disrupted. Emerging markets and developing economies (EMDEs) are expected to shrink by two and a half percent this year, their first contraction as a group in at least sixty years. Per capita incomes are expected to decline by 3.6 percent, which will tip millions of people into extreme poverty this year.[20] Furthermore, the remittance money that millions of foreign workers send home to their dependent families in the developing world are projected to fall by as much as twenty percent this year, largely due to a fall in wages and job losses.[21]

As the first truly global pandemic in twenty years, one notable feature is how national responses have prevailed over a global one. In an increasingly isolationist world, the US has seen its former global role shrink dramatically, tweet by tweet. When the United States formally withdrew from the World Health Organization, this unilateral measure left people the world over scratching their heads, looking for reasons that might go beyond the impending presidential campaign where the incumbent has seen his approval ratings drop by double digits. It was not so long ago, during the 2014 West African Ebola Epidemic, that a previous US administration put the full weight of its support behind the very same WHO.

With no global Pandemic Playbook, countries and regions of the world are having to go it alone, increasing the uneven response, and like the 1918 Spanish Flu, also increasing the haphazard nature of their control mechanisms. This has brought to light disparities at all levels of society, revealing just how much work remains to be done if we are to prevail in the fight for global health.

This history of pandemics across the last 100 years shows us clearly that the world is a global village. COVID-19 spread across countries in record time in a world that is highly interconnected and globalized. We need to learn from our history, including from this pandemic, and use that history to create foresight and anticipatory planning using the world's collective intelligence. Humanity's ability to proactively respond to and deal with these issues calls for a global capacity to anticipate, model scenarios, and plan on how to rapidly react to these types of crises before they become global pandemics. All of this starts with a knowledge of what we have done in the past, what we have gotten right, and what we have learned from our mistakes.

Chapter 2

COVID-19: A Global Response

An Overview of Global Response to COVID-19

The rate of morbidity and mortality due to COVID-19 demonstrates that the pandemic has taken the world by surprise and found us without the capacity to effectively respond. Epidemiological models suggest that in the absence of interventions to slow the rate of infection, the number of deaths directly attributable to the pandemic across the world could reach 40 million, out of seven billion infected.[22] Given the limitations of their health systems, countries have sought to slow the contagion, initially by closing borders and thereafter, shutting down entire economies, measures that entail enormous economic and social costs.

And, so, the pandemic is breeding twin crises. First, the health crisis, in which the direct effects of the disease are expected to cause loss of lives for hundreds of thousands of people. Second, the economic crisis, in which containment measures initially caused a negative shock to aggregate supply and thereafter to aggregate demand. For Sub-Saharan Africa, the two crises might be compounded by a debt crisis that would further undermine countries' efforts to effectively respond to the pandemic.

The future looks bleak. The pandemic's impacts continue to be felt in over 210 countries worldwide, disrupting the social fabric and impacting how people live, interact and relate, how they conduct their daily business and behave. The economic shocks have left many millions dependent on government relief programs. For the citizens of low-income countries, their hope depends on emergency funding from international institutions such as the World Bank Group and the International Monetary Fund. This chapter explores how various actors in the development space have responded to the unfolding pandemic so far. We will look at the World Health Organization, the World Bank, the International Monetary Fund, regional development banks, philanthropy, the private sector, and finally the response in selected countries.

World Health Organization (WHO)

The World Health Organization works worldwide to promote health, keep the world safe, and serve the vulnerable.[23] Part of this mission is addressing diseases – both non-communicable disease prevention and the elimination and eradication of high-impact communicable diseases.[24] To carry out that mission, the WHO is closely tied to decision-makers: Ministries of Health, government agencies, other government departments at the national level, and influencers such as those in civil society. Unfortunately, this global governance body does not have the resources or support to move forward with a response to the pandemic that is both global and comprehensive.

World Bank Group (WBG)

In response to the call for the World Bank Group to take urgent action, on March 17, 2020, the Board (of which I was a member at that time), approved a Fast Track COVID-19 Facility. The new facility was designed to provide up to US $14 billion in immediate support to assist countries in coping with the impact of the global outbreak. Of this amount, US $6 billion came from the WBG's International Bank for Reconstruction and Development, and focused on addressing the health-related aspects of the outbreak. US $8 billion came from the International Finance Corporation (IFC), the WBG's private sector arm, and the Multilateral Investment Guarantee Agency (MIGA) provided US$ 6.5 to guarantee private investment.

Overall, World Bank Group's response to COVID-19 includes emergency financing, policy advice, and technical assistance, building on existing instruments to support eligible countries in addressing the health-related and broader development impacts of COVID-19. The objective is to assist eligible countries in their efforts to prevent, detect, and respond to the threat posed by COVID-19 and strengthen national systems for public health preparedness. This response needs to be both long- and short-term. It is necessary to address the shortcomings of the current core public health systems in a way that also works toward the long-term agenda of having robust public health preparedness in the future.

The World Bank COVID-19 Response comprises two components:

Component 1: Entails US$4 billion in additional resources, channeled under a global emergency Multi-Phase Approach focusing on immediate health-related support for preparedness, response and recovery.

Component 2: An amount of US$2 billion mobilized through any combination of (i) new stand-alone Investment Project Financing or Development Policy Financing from existing funds; (ii) restructuring existing operations, and (iii) cancellation of undisbursed amounts under existing operations and recommitment under the World Bank COVID-19 Response. Once the countries were able to manage the pandemic, the World Bank moved into a second phase, providing plans to help the countries recover economically, so that a large part of these resources went to support countries' budgets.

In a complex system such as the World Bank, approval for funds could become a barrier. To address this, the approval process for these funds was simplified so that the Regional Vice Presidents could approve up to US$100 million, as well as have the freedom to use a system called "absence of objection basis approval" by the Board for larger amounts. Where this system does not meet the country needs or they differ from what can be accommodated under this system, they can still be addressed as free-standing investment-project financing. This policy for funding has allowed the World Bank to respond flexibly to the needs of countries trying to respond to COVID-19.

As of August 2020, a total of fifteen countries under the Constituency had initiated requests for funds valued at US$400.9 million under the new facility. All the projects were approved and are effective by the end of June 2020. Beyond their respective allocations, countries have the option to fast track up to US$2 billion in additional resources from their country program for new health-related projects to deal with COVID-19 impacts. Countries also can restructure ongoing operations which allows countries to quickly reallocate funds within an existing project to be used for emergency needs. Seven countries under the Constituency have triggered the use of this instrument to the value of US$ 200.6 million.

There are several other methods through which countries that already work with the World Bank can respond to emergency conditions even when their funding was not originally public health related. Three countries have done this to the value of US$167 million.

These systems of allocation of funds allow countries that might otherwise not be able to flexibly respond to COVID-19 to find ways to meet the exigencies of the situation. The short-term goal is to build health responses in order that countries can contain the pandemic in their respective countries. The long-term goal includes the ability to rebuild the recovery mechanisms that have been weakened by the lockdown and the closure of the entire global economy.

The World Bank is also responding to the economic impacts of this pandemic. It has committed US$160 billion to be deployed over the next fifteen months to help countries handle the socioeconomic impact of COVID-19.[25] Three pillars will guide the implementation of the second-phase support: protecting the poor and vulnerable, supporting businesses, and strengthening economic resilience and speed of recovery. The lion's share of the resources will be delivered to member countries through the Development Policy Financing instrument and its variants as well as the Program for Results. These instruments are being given priority in order to facilitate rapid disbursements and, by extension, rapid response to the unfolding effects of the pandemic. It is important to note that all the aspects of this pandemic need to be addressed in order to create a comprehensive response; this includes not just public health, but economic and policy impacts. As we build a Pandemic Playbook, the World Bank's multi-faceted approach and flexibility in changing approvals provides a building block to a strong and adaptive future response.

The International Monetary Fund (IMF)

While the pandemic will leave no region unscathed, its impact on Sub-Saharan Africa could be unprecedented owing to the vulnerabilities inherent in health sectors and government balance sheets of the region. Against this backdrop, development partners, including bilateral and multilateral partners, have mobilized financial and material support to help developing countries cope with the pandemic.

Along with the World Bank, other members of the international community have moved swiftly to contain the rapid spread of COVID-19 in the hopes of alleviating the considerable human suffering and major economic disruption. This pandemic, like climate change and other global threats, calls for international cooperation and a global response. We have seen already that no nation can handle a global pandemic alone. We can see from this pandemic that in the future the specialized organizations with a global reach must help coordinate a global response or we are doomed to repeat the failures of the current pandemic.

The International Monetary Fund acts as the lender of last resort for countries not able to obtain financing elsewhere. It responded expeditiously to the COVID-19 pandemic by enhancing its Emergency Financing Toolkit to US$100 billion. The toolkit includes the Rapid Financing Instrument available to all members, and the Rapid Credit Facility available only to low-income countries eligible for concessional financing. The two instruments are used to support member countries to respond more quickly to their urgent balance of payments needs. What this means is that these funds are not aid in the traditional sense. The Fund also extended debt service relief to 25 member countries eligible for support from the Catastrophe Containment and Relief Trust. This allows the International Monetary Fund to provide grants to eligible low-income countries to cover their International Monetary Fund debt-service obligations after catastrophic natural disasters and major global public health emergencies. Beneficiary countries are expected to use freed-up financial resources for vital emergency medical and other relief efforts in fighting the impact of the pandemic. While the countries will eventually need to continue repaying the money, they are able to use those funds immediately for health care and economic relief.

This range of responses has used whatever tools the IMF has at its disposal to address the financial burden of the epidemic. The resulting combination of loans, debt restructuring and instruments allow countries to avail themselves of whatever program fits. This shows how a global response needs to utilize as many agencies as possible to provide for the needs of individual countries. These terms are built on the basis of the economic strength of each of the International Monetary Fund client countries, with the understanding that the solution will come from the country, and that one size does not fit all.

The G20

The group of 20 wealthiest nations, commonly known as the G20, have unanimously called on bilateral official creditors to suspend debt service payments to eligible countries seeking debt forbearance. These efforts yield what is now known as the G20 Debt Service Suspension Initiative (DSSI), where all official bilateral creditors have agreed to participate. DSSI will allow all eligible countries to suspend debt service payments to official bilateral creditors for a period of six months, up to the end of 2020. Beneficiary countries are expected to use the freed-up resources to contain further spread of the outbreak, protect livelihoods and support recovery. Upon recovery, recipient countries are expected to pay back deferred debt service payments over a period of three years, with a grace period of one year. This is a useful and potentially impactful response because it is understood that a large majority of bilateral debt is owed to the G20 Countries. It was important that this group of powerful nations come together to address the issue of debt at an opportune time during a pandemic. It was also significant as a message to private creditors and to multilateral institutions on the importance of considering debt moratoriums. This message will direct others who are owed money to consider repayment during a pandemic and it sent a positive signal to private creditors and multilateral agencies on the issues of addressing debt moratoriums and debt standstills.

Regional Development Banks

The work of supporting countries through the pandemic with financial assistance was also carried out on a more regional level. Regional Development Banks, which are multilateral financial institutions providing financial and technical assistance for development in low-and middle-income countries within their regions, pledged their aid as well. The financing from these banks is provided through low-interest loans and grants and addresses health and education, infrastructure, public administration, financial and private-sector development, agriculture, and environmental and natural resource management.

In April, the African Development Bank Group created a US$10 billion COVID-19 Response Facility to assist member countries in Africa to fight the pandemic. Facilities are flexible response funds that could also be called assistance or resources. The Facility supports governments as well as the private sector. The Facility comprises US$5.5 billion for sovereign operations in African Development Bank Group countries, and US$3.1 billion for sovereign and regional operations for countries under the African Development Fund, the Bank Group's concessional arm that caters to fragile countries. Support to private sector operations amounted to US$1.35 billion. Prior to creating this this Facility, the African Development Bank Group also launched a record-breaking US$3 billion Fight COVID-19 Social Bond, which is the largest US dollar-denominated social bond ever issued on the international capital market. It has also supported the World Health Organization's efforts in its work on the African continent by providing a grant in the amount of US $2 million.

For the Americas, the Inter-America Development Bank (IDB) took unprecedented steps to support its member countries in responding to the pandemic. It has so far mobilized up to US$15 billion in disbursements to respond to the crisis and raised about US$1billion in the issuance of public bonds in US dollars. On the other hand, IDB Invest (the private sector arm of the IDB Group) is expected to spend up to US$5 billion in supporting private sector clients affected by the pandemic.[26] Of this amount, US$4.5 billion from the investment program is directed to support companies impacted by the pandemic, and US$500 million from the Crisis Mitigation Facility targets investments providing a direct response to the pandemic through health and health-related sectors.

The Asian Development Bank (ADB) supported COVID-19 response in the Asia and Pacific Region with an assistance package of US $20 billion. As of end-July, the regional bank had already committed US$9.3 billion of that amount.[27] Additional financing by development partners amounted to US$4.6 billion for the region. To ensure its member countries get the resources needed on time, ADB adjusted its business processes and widened eligibility and scope of various support facilities.

In Europe, the European Bank for Reconstruction and Development (EBRD) has established a €21 billion Coronavirus Solidarity Package to support its 38 emerging economies in dealing with the pandemic's economic impact.[28] Through its Resilience Framework, the package supports EBRD's existing clients by providing up to €4 million to meet the short-term liquidity and working capital. Interestingly, frameworks will be established to reach small and medium-sized enterprises (SMEs) and corporates that are not EBRD clients, in a move to make the real economies in the region more resilient.

These regional responses are extremely important because if we are going to have any kind of global playbook, it requires coordination and cooperation and each of these institutions will be active players. Each of the regional development groupings will be called upon to bring their expertise, knowledge, resources, and funding to join into the global health system.

Philanthropy and the Private Sector

Support for COVID-19 response was also provided by other actors in the development space, particularly to developing countries in Africa. For example, the Jack Ma Foundation and Alibaba Foundation committed to supporting 54 African countries with medical supplies, including testing kits, masks and protective suits. Jack Ma had reportedly committed to providing to each African country 20,000 testing kits, 100,000 masks, and 1,000 medical use protective suits and face shields.[29]

The Bill and Melinda Gates Foundation also committed about US $250 million in support of the global response to COVID-19. Part of this commitment, US $150 million, is expected to finance "the development of diagnostics, therapeutics, vaccines, as well as to provide partners in African and South Asia with resources needed to scale their COVID-19 detection, treatment and isolation efforts."[30] These activities are folded into four priority areas of the Foundation's response to COVID-19: (a) accelerating virus detection; (b) protecting the most vulnerable; (c) minimizing social and economic impact; (d) developing products for a sustainable response. These are only a few representative philanthropies and corporates out of many that are making an enormous contribution to the fight against the pandemic.

These philanthropic and private sector organizations, which we will refer to later as part of the group of non-state actors, highlight that there is a range of groups outside of the already existing financial structures that have significant funds available, and so must be part of the global playbook. Their assistance is vital, and it needs to be coordinated so that their impact is as large as possible in the places where it is most needed.

National Government Responses of Selected Countries

Governments of different countries have taken emergency steps to bailout various economic sectors by borrowing a page from previous recessions. In responding to COVID-19, the United States of America has advanced a US $2.3 trillion[31] stimulus package under the Coronavirus Aid, Relief and Economy Security Act ("CARES Act").[32] This package provided one-time tax rebates to individuals; expanded unemployment benefits; provided a food safety net for the most vulnerable; prevented corporate bankruptcy by providing loans and guarantees; forgave small business administration loans and guaranteed to help small businesses that retain workers; supported hospitals;

and gave cash transfers to state and local governments and international assistance. The United States also responded by implementing two other packages: a US $483 billion Paycheck Protection Program and Health Care Enhancement Act; US $8.3 billion Coronavirus Preparedness and Response Supplemental Appropriations Act; and US$192 billion Families First Coronavirus Response Act.

In the United Kingdom, the government implemented various fiscal measures aimed at first responding to the health crisis and then supporting companies' recovery. These measures are expected to provide additional funding of about £85.5 billion. It has put in place a £1 billion package to support companies driving innovation and development through loans and grants. In supporting the international response, the government contributed £150 million to the IMF's Catastrophe Containment and Relief Trust. It provided a new £2.2 billion loan to the IMF Poverty Reduction and Growth Trust (PRGT) to help low-income countries respond to COVID-19.

The Chinese government has implemented an estimated RMB 4.6 trillion (about US $668 billion) of discretionary fiscal measures which aim to increase spending on prevention and control of the pandemic, production of medical equipment, accelerating disbursement of unemployment insurance and extension to migrant workers, tax relief and waived social security contributions, as well as ramping up public investment. This is equivalent to 4.5 percent of China's GDP. On the other side, monetary policy remained accommodative to support businesses.

In South Korea, a series of fiscal measures was put in place to cushion its economy and the population from the virus's impact. First, the National Assembly approved KRW 10.9 trillion or approximately US $9 billion additional spending on disease prevention and prevention and support to businesses affected. Second, the Assembly approved the second supplementary budget, including an increase in spending by KRW 8 trillion to finance an emergency relief payment program of KRW 14.3 trillion, which provides transfers to households. Third, it unveiled a KRW 35.1 trillion package composed of revenue reduction (KRW 11.4 trillion) and additional 23.7 trillion spending on financial support for companies, expansion of employment and social safety, disease control, and spending on digital and green industries. Finally, monetary policy remained accommodative and facilitated the liquidity needs of businesses.

Brazilian Authorities have taken a host of fiscal measures adding up to 11.8 percent of GDP. This package aims to provide temporary income support to vulnerable households, employment support, lower tax breaks and import levies on essential medical supplies, and a new transfer to state governments to support higher health spending and cushion against the expected fall in revenues.

As an example of individual countries' expenditures, of the US$1.7 billion that the World Health Organization estimated as required to respond to COVID-19 until December 2020, it has thus far received $907,603,481. Of that amount, in round figures, the World Bank supplied $47 million and the World Bank/PEF $21 million. The biggest donor in terms of countries were the UK at $110 million and Germany at $93 million, followed by Kuwait and Japan, respectively at $60 million and $50.6 million. Of note is the AfDB's donation of $16.5 million. Two other African Countries, Côte d'Ivoire and Guinea issued donations totaling less than a million dollars.[33]

In other African countries, it is estimated that the continent needs about $100 billion in funding for an effective response to COVID-19. On average each country in Africa is spending 1.07% of their GDP to respond to COVID19, adding up to roughly US$ 37.8 billion. However, this average is a distorted picture as reportedly approximately 85% of that amount is from South-Africa and Nigeria.[34]

While all of these nation-state responses should be applauded and have definitely made a difference, their range of responses and the disparities between them and lack of ongoing coordination are an indication that pandemic response cannot be adequately met by a nation-state approach. A global pandemic should be handled as a global problem in order for the results to be more effective, long lasting, and for success stories to be passed on from one region to another.

Costly Coordination Failure

What we are learning from the preceding responses against the COVID-19 pandemic is that there are commitments from various stakeholders to make the world a safer place for every human being. However, the scale and scope of the responses differ, and this difference is stark between developed and developing countries. To cut the story short, we are witnessing a costly coordination failure whose undesirable outcomes are likely to be felt by countries in the developing world due to their weak financial and technical capacity to respond effectively to the pandemic. This coordination failure is attested by the Bill and Melinda Gates Foundation in their statement that "[T]here is not yet a global consensus on the total resources required to turn back COVID-19." Since our approach is rooted in the nation-state, we are essentially doomed to fail miserably.

When countries embrace the nationalist approach in fighting a global public ill like COVID-19, we unnecessarily set ourselves up for a long fight, and stack the odds against our success. Let's recall the lessons of the 1918 Spanish Flu pandemic and the recent Ebola Virus outbreak: During Ebola there was a coordinated global response that took into consideration public health and policy and economics, and the disease was contained. During the Spanish Flu there was no globally coordinated effort, and the outcome was devastating.

Notwithstanding the rich epidemiological history

bequeathed to us from the previous century, information sharing by countries has unfortunately been haphazard, some deliberately and some due to weak biostatistics systems. In procuring essential personal protective equipment and other medical supplies, we have witnessed uncomfortable outbidding not only among rich countries but sadly between rich and developed countries, and, at the extreme, among states within the same country. In response to COVID-19, some countries are implementing huge stimulus packages while others cannot. While some are under lockdown, others have rejected the science or listening to experts. On top of all these shortcomings, evidence emerging from countries at all levels of the income spectrum demonstrates that the existing national health systems and infrastructure are simply inadequate to deal with the pandemic of the type of COVID-19. As we move forward, we must keep in mind that individual nations, even the richest on the planet, are not capable of dealing with a global pandemic independently. We live in a globally connected world and our response to pandemic disease must follow suit. This Global Pandemic Playbook idea only works if everyone comes into a well-coordinated system with their knowledge and resources. It requires that the regional groups, the nation states, the private sector, the philanthropic organization do not approach the solutions on their own, but can coordinate and collaborate a response to protect our one global "home."

Chapter 3

The Case for Change

The Costs of the Pandemic

The COVID-19 pandemic is exacting an unprecedented human toll. By the end of August 2020, confirmed cases globally reached over 25 million and reported deaths hit over 838 thousand. Doubtless, it will cross the one million mark by the time this book is published. Over half of the infected and deceased are from the Americas and Western Pacific. Africa remains the least affected region in terms of both mortality and morbidity but this is rising at an increasing rate. Despite the human toll, the pandemic is associated with other social impacts as well. The disruption of the education systems is the largest in history, affecting nearly 1.6 billion learners in more than 190 countries across all continents.[35]

Additionally, closure of schools and other learning institutions has impacted 94 percent of the world's student population, the rate that goes up to 99 percent in lower-and lower-middle-income countries. The crisis could potentially exacerbate pre-existing education disparities by curtailing the opportunities for many of the most vulnerable children. It is estimated that about 23.8 million additional children and youth may drop out or not have access to school next year.[36] In countries and localities that are relying on online education, the lack of computers and electronic devices for the most vulnerable students exacerbates already existing disparities. Sadly, this presents disturbing regression from the enormous progress towards human capital development, particularly in low and lower-middle-income countries.

COVID-19, like previous outbreaks, exposes and compounds forces of marginalization along the lines of gender, race, caste and class.[37] Women more than men are likely to bear the brunt of the unfolding crisis, and so are their lives and livelihoods. Available evidence suggests that in low and middle-income nations, the cutback in maternal care during COVID-19 could claim the lives of up to 113,000 women. Early estimates also suggest the pandemic will cause 49 million additional women to go without contraceptives, leading to 15 million additional unplanned pregnancies. Early estimates suggest that around the world, women's jobs are 1.8 times as likely to be cut in this recession than jobs held by men. Before the pandemic began, unpaid work was already a major barrier to women's economic equality. Now, with many schools closed and health systems overwhelmed, more women may be forced to leave the workforce altogether. If the pandemic stalls progress toward gender equality, the cost will be in the trillions of dollars. Even a four-year wait in taking new action to improve parity – for example, by introducing interventions to advance women's digital and financial inclusion – would erase $5 trillion in opportunity from global GDP in 2030. As policymakers work to protect and rebuild economies, their response must account for the disproportionate impact of COVID-19 on women – and the unique roles women will have to play in mitigating the pandemic's harm. Finally, accelerated digitalization during and in the aftermath of the COVID-19 pandemic is likely to foment the digital divide, as women in the developing world are ten percent less likely to own a phone than men, which means that 313 million fewer women than men use mobile internet.

The global economy is projected to contract by 4.9 percent in 2020, as the COVID-19 pandemic has had a more negative impact on activities in the first half of 2020 than anticipated, and the recovery is projected to be more gradual than previously forecast. Advanced economies as a group are projected to contract by 8.0 percent in 2020 as voluntary social distancing measures prevail, and fear of contagion is likely to continue.

These economies are projected to experience synchronized deep downturns in 2020, before recovering with a growth of 4.8 percent in 2021. In 2021 global growth is projected at 5.4 percent.

Emerging markets and developing economies will suffer because COVID-19 will weaken demand. These emerging market economies are expected to contract by three percent overall and if you take out China's economy the prediction is closer to five percent. Within these Emerging Markets and Developing Economies, growth among low-income countries is projected to contract by one percent. The adverse impact of the COVID-19 induced slowdown on low-income households is particularly acute, imperiling the significant progress made in reducing extreme poverty in the world since the 1990s.

All regions are expected to post negative growth in 2020, albeit with substantial differences across individual economies, reflecting the evolution of the pandemic and the effectiveness of containment strategies, variation in economic structure, reliance on external financial flows, including remittances; and precise growth trends. These differences highlight the differences in individual responses. If we were to have a Global Pandemic Playbook, we may in the future be able to create a more equitable system.

The expected decline in remittance flows – the money that workers laboring in foreign countries are able to send home – will weigh on human development. Remittance flows are projected to fall by 20 percent in 2020, down by US$109 billion from US$554 billion last year. This fall will deny many families the financial support they need to live even at the most basic levels. Remittance flows to Africa and South Asia in 2020 is projected to fall by 23 percent and 22 percent, respectively, while in East Asia and the Pacific it will fall by thirteen percent in 2020. Importantly, remittances account for a remarkable percent of the GDP in developing countries (8.9 percent in 2019), and in small island developing states (7.7 percent), and for those countries in fragile and conflict-affected situations (9.2 percent). The pandemic is severely impacting the world of work, with four out of five people in the global workforce affected by full or partial pandemic-related workplace closures.[38] Nearly 80 percent of the world's informal economy workers who work jobs outside the formal economy who are not taxed or formally tracked – 1.6 billion people – have faced COVID-19 lockdowns and slowdowns in hard-hit sectors. About four in ten young people employed globally were working in hard-hit sectors when the crisis began, further complicating the challenge of youth unemployment. As the informal sector accounts for up to 90 percent of workers in some emerging economies, the implications of lost wages will cascade from households to communities to entire societies. Additionally, about 77 percent of the world's young workers were in informal jobs, compared with around 60 percent of adult workers. According to the International Labor Organization (ILO), the youth informality rate is, unfortunately, the highest in Africa, at 93.4 percent. A prolonged and widespread crisis in EMDEs could force firms to scale back further, including more layoffs and/or reduced compensation. A collapse of firms will break relations with workers that will be difficult to restore quickly once recovery begins.

175 million more people are now projected to be poor in 2020 (at the US$3.20 per day poverty line), many of them newly poor. The pandemic will also entrap millions of people in extreme poverty, inflicting deep deprivation upon them. The World Bank's Global Economic Prospects indicates that 73 million more people could be living in extreme poverty in 2020: the first increase in global poverty since 1998. Nearly one-half of these would be in South Asia and one-third in Sub-Saharan Africa. This will mean an estimated additional 18 million destitute people in Fragile and Conflict States (FCS) countries. Extreme

poverty is likely to persist at these higher levels in 2021 and potentially beyond.

The coronavirus pandemic could cost the global economy between US$5.8 trillion according to the Asian Development Bank and US$15.8 trillion according to the World Economic Forum. In contrast, it would cost the world between $22.2 and $30.7 billion each year to significantly reduce transmission of new diseases from tropical forests according to the World Economic Forum.

By all standards, the COVID-19 is exacting unprecedented health, social and economic impacts. However, the crisis presents a unique opportunity for the international community to install a new system or overhaul the existing framework so that we may be able to effectively address future pandemics. An account of the impacts above demonstrates that we were not able to leverage the opportunities presented by the previous pandemics to future-proof our institutions that were supposed to protect us. Frequent recurrence of pandemics in recent years should be a wake-up call and remind us that whatever development endeavors we aim to pursue would be meaningless if we live in constant fear of the next pandemic.

Chapter 4

Towards a Global Playbook for Pandemics

The world was caught flat-footed as coronavirus disease (COVID-19) infected more than 20 million people and caused over 850,000 deaths (as of August 2020). Sadly, this catastrophic human impact happened after the public health community warned us that the next major pandemic was on the way; it was a matter not of "if" but of "when." What we are unwittingly experiencing today is, to no small extent, an outcome of complacency.

Medical professionals have repeatedly shown that no nation, rich or poor, was fully prepared to contain infectious diseases and mitigate their impacts. The 2019 assessment by the Global Health Security Alliance is case in point. Their findings include this statement: "The GHS Index analysis finds no country is fully prepared for epidemics or pandemics. Collectively, international preparedness is weak. Many countries do not show evidence of the health security capacities and capabilities that are needed to prevent, detect, and respond to significant infectious disease outbreaks."[39]

It is also sad that this devastation of our social fabric is happening not in the nineteenth or twentieth century, but the twenty-first century in which humanity has attained the highest level of civilization, a time of remarkable advances in medical science and its affiliate fields, as well as a stronger international cooperation and robust global connectivity. Yet, we haplessly allow our fellow human beings to perish from pestilence.

An in-depth review of the global response in Chapter 2 indicates the response has been nothing but chaotic with underwhelming international cooperation and collaboration, to the extent that nationalist responses to the pandemic have occasionally strained relationships between nations. Six months into the crisis, and despite the urgency of unfolding human catastrophe and the immediacy of economic collapse we are witnessing, there has still been no moment where nations have been convened to reflect on lessons to be learned, to coordinate actions to protect citizens, and to plan for future spikes or waves of infection.

This avoidable loss of life and well-being should be an urgent wake-up call to every nation, institution, and individual, and, most importantly, to the international community. This call is well elaborated by Debora Mackenzie in *The Pandemic That Never Should Have Happened:*

> We cannot let a virus catch our interconnected global community this stupidly flat-footed again. We cannot let it break those interconnections either, at least not all of them. If this pandemic teaches us anything, it is that up against a contagious disease, we are all in this together. One big early lesson was that no country can really seal off their borders anymore or go it alone. Our society is global; our risk is global; our response and our cooperation must be global.[40]

We can clearly see what a functional global health system should be doing better during pandemics by looking at what our existing system has failed to do well in this one. Additions to the current global health architecture must be built if we are to better contain an even more life-threatening pandemic. Indeed, the response to the current pandemic is still evolving, and countries or the international community might eventually correct course. The contents of this chapter are thus largely based on the state of our systems as the time of writing (August 2020).

Global Health Governance

This pandemic revealed with acute clarity the injustices and inequities in our public health system. One striking example is the harsh economic impact of lockdowns on people who barely survive on precarious livelihoods. About two billion people make their living in the informal economy, and over 90 percent of them live in low-income and low-middle-income countries. The informal economy is comprised of jobs not taxed or traced by government bodies. This means they are often not the recipients of economic stimulus because their work is invisible. Hunger is an immediate direct threat to these people and their families, both due to the loss of daily wages and the disruption of food supply chains. The United Nations has estimated that over 300 million children who rely on school meals for most of their nutritional needs might now be at risk of acute hunger, which could reverse in a year the progress made over the past two to three years in reducing infant mortality. The bottom line is that the problem of pandemics cannot be sufficiently addressed without talking about global inequality.

The breakdown of the governance structure of the global public health was also vividly manifested by the lack of global public health infrastructure to ensure every country's response was adequate, even though inadequate response in any country could mean increased infection in others. Sadly, no crisis-management systems were in place to counteract local or national governments' denial and delay, even as this negligence affected everyone. Denying the science of pandemics at the highest levels of some national governments did an intolerable disservice to the international efforts deliberately devoted to containing the pandemic and its impacts. We need a better system that would minimize the heartbreaking culture of compromising scientific evidence with undue secrecy, ideology or wishful thinking.

While there is currently some disease surveillance, unfortunately most of it does not happen in high-risk environments such as tropical Africa, China or India. Instead, it happens where the money and scientists are, in rich, temperate-climate countries.[41] This needs to be fixed, urgently. We need to scale up disease surveillance in countries with zoonoses (disease or infection that is naturally transmissible from vertebrate animals to humans) hotspots and this exercise could start immediately with the World Health Organization's list of worrying viruses, of which coronavirus is one form. The surveillance systems would help us detect, trace, respond to and prevent any rapidly spreading virus with lethal potency.

The world (through the International Monetary Fund) conducts routine economic surveillance in systemically important countries with the view of ensuring that no one country's policies, or lack of them, poses significant risks to the stability of the global financial system. We should have a similar system in the space of public health since, as we have vividly witnessed in the wake of COVID-19, even the global financial system tends to be fragile in the wake of a pandemic. That said, welfare gains from investing in disease surveillance might be even larger than what we realize currently with economic surveillance.

Current and future global challenges demand far better international cooperation and significantly more decisive action to avoid worst-case scenarios. Given the lack of action by important international political bodies in dealing with COVID-19, and the impacts of that lack of action, efforts and resources ought to be channeled to more flexible international organizations who have the knowledge, access, and proven ability to provide rapid response to unfolding events. The new structure will need to be guided by new rules that allow program flexibility and move away from the bureaucracy that has been built into our current organizations since their creation in 1945. Considering that such organizations are not hermetically sealed off from the political environments in which they exist and operate, reforms that improve transparency and mechanisms to demand accountability on critical decisions need to be in place in local governments. Although the competition between the great global political powers is likely to be a feature of global dynamics for the foreseeable future, such steps would contribute to minimizing the risks of the dysfunction we experienced and found was reinforced by the current international response to COVID-19.

The World Health Organization had reportedly planned to roll out routine disease surveillance in pathogen hotspots in the aftermath of Ebola Virus disease outbreak in West Africa. However, these surveillances could not be done due to lack of funding. This, again, reflects collective failure by the international community to prioritize public health and invest in preparedness, especially at a time when the WHO is being expected to do even more: it has acquired an emergency response capability, expanded its work on antibiotic resistance and the health threats of climate change, and almost completed polio eradication. If the global community is to throw its weight behind the World Health Organization as the guardian of global public health, its financing mechanism need to be overhauled to ensure it has predictable funding for the long term – as some of its scientific engagements, such as investing in research and development of vaccines, are long-term projects. Without an increased and predictable WHO funding, the world will remain unprepared for future pandemics. WHO is only as strong and effective at its members allow and support it to be. Criticism about its role in managing COVID-19 therefore needs to be assessed against the measures its members have taken to strengthen and capacitate it to fulfill its mandate.

For most developing countries it will be difficult to improve their health care systems to a standard similar to that of high-income countries. Moreover, as mentioned, most low- and middle-income countries will not be able to establish core

"International Health Regulations" capabilities without considerable donor support and international assistance for training, creating the necessary laboratory infrastructure for prompt diagnosis, and the technology required for "real-time" reporting of epidemics. Luckily, point-of-care screening tests for use in community health is increasingly available for rapid diagnosis of emerging pathogens and will shorten the time from presentation to treatment, even as a majority of these elements failed in a majority of the countries impacted by COVID-19, globally. However, where the resources were sufficient, such as in Germany, some of these elements were introduced and were successful in containing COVID-19. The need to holistically use a range of these elements across the globe to serve a greater number of countries will be essential for successful pandemic response in the future. Improvements and access to diagnostic technologies will need to be supported by the ability to interpret and act upon the findings. This pandemic has unveiled the fact that developing countries, as well as developed countries, lack three of the essential parts of what constitutes a functional health system: personnel, infrastructure, and medical supplies. In fact, the dysfunctionality of health systems was more evident in some developed countries due to the severity of the COVID-19 infections there; the situation in developing countries could have been much worse had they faced the same levels of contagion.

The pandemic also serves as a reminder that health security is critical to national security. Countries with weak health systems are poorly equipped to mount a strong defense against the massive onslaught of an unseen enemy. The COVID-19 pandemic should be leveraging to explore long-term investment needed to have pandemic-resilient health systems in developing countries, not only for the improvement of improved basic health-care services, but also strengthening the economic resilience of these countries.

International Collaboration and Coordination

Recent past pandemics, starting from Ebola in West Africa to Zika in South America to MERS in the Middle East, have all taught us that sharing information, early and accurately, is the first line of defense in preventing any outbreak from becoming a pandemic. However, there are indications that there was slippage in applying this lesson during the early days of the COVID-19 outbreak, when one local bureaucracy delayed the warning – and there was no international agency that could go in and verify what was happening on the ground, immediately, on behalf of everyone else.[42] Reports from various sources agree with the assessment of the New York Times that "officials in the city of Wuhan and in Hubei Province, where the outbreak began late last year, tried to hide information from China's central leadership. The finding is consistent with reporting by news organizations and with assessments by China's experts of the country's opaque governance system."[43]

Consequently, the virus hopped a plane out of Wuhan and traveled "round the world." Against this backdrop, it is clear that there is a need to have a high-level, authoritative system that is capable of bringing countries and international agencies together to collaborate on disease. These large systematic changes are needed to help us respond more efficiently and effectively when the next pandemic arrives. This system would ensure information asymmetry and coordination failure with the governance structure of global public health are warded off, by obligating countries with outbreaks to share important details.

To date, the pandemic has revealed that global distribution chains, despite their merits (especially of medical supplies and personal protective equipment), do not work when situations are far from ideal. Over the last couple of years, nations have increasingly become more reliant on a few countries for the supplies of critical drugs and medical supplies. This trend poses risks to the ability of nations to effectively respond to pandemics since factories or shipping services could be shut down in the countries where these supplies are produced should there be a local outbreak or natural disaster. To avoid the scrambling for critical drugs and scarce medical supplies we witnessed during the COVID-19 pandemic, two options can be pursued. First, individual countries may choose to have a repository of allocated medical equipment that can quickly be used to meet the demand for pandemics. Second, a group of countries could decide to regionalize distribution and supply chains of essential medical supplies and periodically evaluate regional industries' capabilities to adequately supply their regional members in the wake of pandemic. These issues should be factored in as countries are looking forward to boosting capabilities of their health systems in responding to pandemics.

Foresight, Anticipation, Early Warning and Speedy Response

Scientific research shows a clear association between disease outbreaks and climate change. This means we are entering an era when pandemics like COVID-19 will become commonplace. Additionally, as our population increases, we need to clear more land for our habitat. The processes of deforestation and clearing land brings us closer to wildlife, which is the main reservoir of infectious pathogens. Available evidence suggests that COVID-19 as well as the deadly Ebola virus disease were caused by the jumping of the respective virus from wildlife to human being, an event virologists call "zoonosis." This trend will continue as long as population growth increases, and people need land on which to live. Because of this trend, and the experience of COVID-19 unpreparedness, we need to institute disease surveillance systems that will help spot clusters of cases early and be able to contain the infectious pathogen. In the wake of an Ebola virus outbreak in West Africa, we knew there was a need to be prepared, and yet we were not.

Scientists predict that the next pandemic is likely to be of influenza type, so the development of influenza vaccines at a scale that would allow vaccination of the world's population would be game changing. Again, this was the lost opportunity from past pandemics, such as SARS. In its aftermath, we should have started developing a list of vaccines to prepare for similar influenza pandemics. This could save us weeks or even months after a future influenza outbreak. While this endeavor would entail a huge cost and enormous effort, the savings of averting a pandemic would be justified many times over. This goal is attainable – just like the eradication of smallpox. But it needs the creative imagination of our best scientists, the visionary support of our policy leaders, technological and financial commitment, and the necessary project-management structure. Joint efforts from national governments, philanthropic organizations, vaccine manufacturers, and the WHO would be to work together to make it happen.

The onset of the current pandemic and its unprecedented global impact has awakened the appetite for vaccines like never before. At the time of this writing, about 170 vaccines were at various stages of development, with a few frontrunners entering stage-three trials. This is really a welcome development. However, the funding for these efforts so far has been uneven and uncoordinated, and countries are not responding to the need for vaccines with equal concern for efficacy and safety. The Coalition for Epidemic Preparedness Innovation seems to be the right vehicle to finance independent research projects to develop vaccines against emerging infectious diseases and to oversee this process so that we are prepared with safe and effective vaccine options. Despite the good prospects in the realm of vaccine development, many big questions remain. Have the funders agreed to equitable access? How will the vaccines be priced? Will governments commit to sharing vaccines according to fair allocation rules being developed by WHO? Can technology be transferred royalty-free to multiple manufacturers? The question of who will get priority access to vaccines is core to the global public interest. We need to get the governance of these decisions right. Otherwise there will be tremendous resentment and unnecessary deaths, not to mention decreased capacity to get the pandemic under control.

Transparency in such decisions is fundamental. It is imperative that more governments and pharmaceutical companies agree to shoulder the costs of vaccine research and manufacturing, and to share data and technologies. They need to commit to WHO allocation guidelines and cooperate globally to distribute vaccines fairly to those at greatest risk. A pandemic vaccine needs strong global governance behind it to ensure that, according to Bill Gates, we can develop safe, effective vaccines and antivirals, get them approved, and deliver billions of doses within a few months after the discovery of a fast-moving pathogen.[44]

In addition to a disease surveillance system, we need to improve our systems for monitoring and response by leveraging technologies such as the computerized alert system that China installed after SARS and contact tracing apps that are increasingly becoming available. These technologies could be rolled out in zoonosis hotspots where the risk of hyper-infectious diseases is greatest. Once this system exists, we must make sure that disease alerts are widely and timely shared by medical professionals while ensuring privacy of information providers.

Since pandemic outbreaks and climate change are intricately linked, any system meant to steer long-term pandemic preparedness plans should help us mainstream climate change as one of the accelerators of pathogen outbreaks. Establishing this link would provide an avenue for experts from the poor, middle income, and rich countries to easily share information and thus detect any health anomaly in animal and human health – and then act.

While there is innovation globally, even, and sometimes especially, by poor countries around pandemics like Ebola, the innovation and expertise cannot be harnessed as long as the responses are local or regional. As long as we maintain a system that is both uneven, and often reinforces the inequities suffered by poor and middle-income countries, no one will be safe from the ravages of the next pandemic. There is no question there will indeed be a next one. The only question is, will we be prepared?

Chapter 5

The World Bank and the Global Pandemic Playbook

What would our mindset be towards pandemics if we took their inevitability seriously? That is, if we truly accepted the increasing frequency with which diseases will jump from wildlife to humans, and how vulnerable our societies are to the health and economic crises caused by such jumps. Said differently, what would it be like if we were prepared for rolling and ongoing pandemics that keep coming back and are going to get bigger as our planet gets hotter and more crowded?

In the previous chapters we learned that scientifically recommended measures to contain the spread of virus outbreaks were almost universal: social distancing, lockdowns, closure of international airports and so on. While proven effective at slowing down the pace of the outbreak, the pandemic-containment measures' impact on people's livelihoods turned out to be starkly different in developing and developed countries. As the majority of the world's poor people are clustered just above the poverty line, the recent pandemic-induced health and economic shocks are expected to push at least 49 million people into poverty, eliminating nearly all the economic and social gains made since 2017. Since people in developing countries earn their livelihoods mainly in the informal economy, when pandemic-containment measures shut these enterprises down, *somebody* has to provide for these vulnerable workers. This would only be possible if developing countries had universal social protection – which they don't. Or, if as in advanced countries, their governments had the budget space so they could pay vulnerable citizens during the lockdowns and curfews – which they can't.

It is clear, then, that pandemics threaten to undo decades of development gains. Gains that countries, with the support of the international community, have been able to achieve through programs like the United Nations Sustainable Development Goals. To be more specific, COVID-19 undercuts the mission of any organization bent on eradicating poverty and boosting shared prosperity. What does this mean in practice? Simply that public health, including pandemic preparedness, should be part and parcel of any development strategy. This is essential if hard-won development gains are to be safeguarded and sustainable.

The argument in this chapter is that the World Bank Group has a clear grasp of the intertwined relationship between poverty and public health, making it one of the four key players in the field of global public health, along with the WHO, GAVI (the World Vaccine Alliance), and Global Fund, a partnership designed to accelerate the end of AIDS, tuberculosis and malaria as epidemics. It is on this basis that I believe the World Bank Group must recognize and take up its role as a leader on global health issues. The alternative poses a threat to its mission and, ultimately, its legitimacy. Responding to pandemics and disaster prevention is one of the issues that the World Bank should be leading to stay true to its mission. It is no longer possible to look through the lens of economic development without seeing public health as a foundation upon which that development depends.

Besides helping developing countries with the financial resources and technical assistance needed to strengthen health systems and improve access to quality health services, the World Bank has put in place a Crisis Response Window to support these countries during the slower-onset crises for disease outbreaks and food insecurity. The World Bank has used this facility to support countries to respond to the health crisis brought by COVID-19. But there remains a need for the Bank to broaden the scope of its strategy for dealing with pandemics in a holistic way beyond the current setup, which relies on Trust Funds and the Crisis Response Window.

We have repeatedly heard from the scientific community that the current pandemic is a harbinger of disasters yet to come that will have local, regional, and global repercussions. In this regard, the objective of this chapter is to explore how the World Bank can position itself better to provide leadership on global public health – which, as argued above, is at the very core of its development mission.

The proposal is made with a clear recognition that the global health architecture is increasingly diverse and complex, as it includes not just global health and economic institutions but governments and non-state actors comprising everyone from corporations to religious groups, non-governmental organizations, aid agencies, lobbying groups, and even the media. The rest of this chapter will explore the structure and proposed solution to this pressing question: What do we need to do to be ready when the next pandemic hits? And more specifically: How can the World Bank be the coordinator of the Global Pandemic Playbook?

We will first review the existing structures within the World Bank that create the possibility of success in this endeavor. We will then, in the final chapter consider the ways in which this can be accomplished in concert with the other global players who have responded to COVID-19, facilitated by the World Bank's coordination, unification and direction.

Structure, Financing and Strategy

In order to build a foundation for global pandemic response and resilient global health systems that can withstand next pandemics, we urgently need a holistic framework that leverages the plethora of state and non-state actors and consolidates fragmented pockets of resources. The World Bank, as one of the primary international actors on global health, has put in place the Pandemic and Emergency Facility and Crisis Response Window as responses to the onset crisis. It specifically underscores urgency and pertinence for the World Bank to renew its focus on how it supports low- and middle-income countries' health systems to be pandemic resilient, or at least minimize their glaring weaknesses exposed by the COVID-19 pandemic.

The World Bank's pandemic toolkit begins with the response to COVID-10 using the already existing Crisis Response Window that though it was undoubtedly designed for pandemics or disasters at the country or a sub-regional level, allowed the response to be quick and broad on a regional level. The Crisis Response Window needs to be broadened to include a global level of response for future pandemics. This is the structure which the World Bank Group can readily and immediately use to unify and solidify pandemic responses.

Alternatively, the Bank can use its current extensive focus on dealing and responding to this particular pandemic by extending and strengthening its Health, Nutrition, and Population Global Practice. If nothing else, the COVID-19 pandemic has taught us all where our weak spots are and where our pandemic response could be strengthened, and with that information and decisive action, the World Bank could substantially contribute to making the global health system resilient and effective.

Country-Level Preparedness

First, preparedness for a pandemic requires building a resilient health system at the country level. We have learned from past outbreaks that this is the building block for a strong and swift response. This activity already directly falls under the purview of the World Bank's project and policy lending. The current pandemic, as well as the last few pandemics, have laid bare that health systems in most, if not all, developing countries tend to get overwhelmed in the event of outbreaks due to the lack of medical personnel, medical equipment and supplies. To be able to strengthen health systems for unknown pathogens effectively, the World Bank should do two things:

1. Consider creating a new entity that would handle its services in human capital responses, meaning those that include and incorporate the COVID-19 pandemic lessons: nutrition, population education, health, and everything that is considered Human Capital Development.

2. The World Health Organization's list of most-likely pathogens should be used to identify the kind of health systems that would be needed in the event of an outbreak. This list is large since the worldwide number of potential pathogens is large and the resources currently available are limited. One of the diseases on that list, along with COVID-19, Ebola and SARS, is "Disease X." This is the acknowledgement that another global pandemic could be caused by a pathogen we don't yet know or follow. Our preparedness, as discussed, should cover all potential pandemic diseases – the known and the unknown.

It is through this sector-wide approach that the World Bank can prove invaluable in preparing the global health systems for the next pandemic. While there are many other actors in the field of pandemic containment and responses, they are usually either disease-focused or nation-state focused and are not likely to have long-term commitments to the overall health sector.

Second, having a resilient health system is necessary, but accessibility to quality health service is also crucial. The World Bank's commitment to helping its client countries achieve the Sustainable Development Goals targets for universal health coverage is another comparative advantage that the World Bank holds in the global health landscape. Executed well, universal health coverage has the potential to build to the resilience of health systems by addressing the declining financial protection and persistent gaps in health equity, thereby assuring health care for all members of society.

Third, a state is a primary custodian of citizens' health, and its capacity to sufficiently allocate resources to the health sector is vitally important. In their development plans, all national states aim to build an infrastructure capable of both public health activities (such as information-gathering and surveillance) as well as delivering comprehensive health services to their populations today and in the future. The Bank, through its long-term relationship with ministries of finance and health, is uniquely positioned as a trusted broker to influence investments and reforms in the health sector. Leveraging its near-universal membership, the World Bank, therefore, plays critical roles in modernizing and strengthening the health sector across its global membership.

The World Bank is, therefore, best placed to help states invest in health services because health outcomes depend not only on health policy and financing but on what happens in other sectors that are the purview of the state and are natural areas of assistance for none but the World Bank Group. That said, the Bank's support to states not only in health but related sectors provides a comparative advantage over other players in the global health landscape for building resilient health systems.

The Bank's engagement with client countries in the health sector has recently gained prominence among developing countries thanks to the launch of the Human Capital Initiative, and the Initiative's Human Capital Index. The index measures the amount of human capital that a child born today in a specific country can expect to achieve, in view of the risks of poor health and poor education currently prevailing in that country.[45] This highlights the productivity losses each country faces due to underinvestment in both health and education.[46] Any new fundraising for this critical international development organization should reflect these human capital measures and their contribution to global public health.

Collaboration, Communication, and Consolidation of Efforts

The World Bank is not the only player in global health governance, with WHO now joined by non-state actors like the GAVI and Global Fund. Ideally, new actors would play a complementary role in the provision of health services. There is, however, currently no clear framework to ensure that the new institutions do not end up replicating the work of existing institutions. The World Bank could leverage a plethora of new actors in the health sector to maximize resources and minimize fragmentation – which has become a clear hazard during the current pandemic. For example, how did the world end up with over 170 COVID-19 vaccines under development, given high sunk costs involved and uncertainty of the efficacy of those vaccines? Ideally, the international community could have come together and pooled resources, and invested wisely in a fraction of the current vaccine candidates. This attempt would have produced quick results and taken less time and fewer resources as well as avoided political pitfalls in individual countries.

Assuming that a future pandemic is being addressed by different actors, whether General Electric helping in the Philippines or the Bill Gates Foundation helping to develop vaccines, the way the World Bank works with both state and non-state actors would need to change in order to support new modes of financing by these new actors. Since the resources mobilized and invested by these actors are sizable, the Bank should find a way to bring them together and leverage economies of scale both in financing and technical issues.

Conclusion

The World Bank has been at the forefront of governing global health since the late 1960s. The current pandemic has, however, revealed that health systems across the globe are inadequate to deal with any pandemic of the scale we have experienced. As the largest financier of health in low–middle-income countries and a leader of global health policy, the World Bank has an opportune moment to reflect on what worked and course-correct what has not worked to help its client countries prepare their health systems for the next pandemic or other global disasters. The Bank has some in-house facilities designed to help countries in the event of outbreaks or disasters. However, those facilities were designed to respond to pandemic/disasters confined to a particular country or sub-region, not occurrences that wreak havoc worldwide. The Bank will need to adapt to maintain its relevance to the practice of global public health at a time when there are many (albeit, uncoordinated), players and when the frequent occurrence of those disasters threaten the Bank's overarching mission: working towards a world free of poverty where everyone enjoys a fair share of the economy. This is an outsize responsibility that should not be left to the Bank alone as it touches on the social fabric of every nation, both in developed and developing countries. While the Bank has comparative advantages in some facets of the global health system, making it holistically resilient would require the World Bank to cooperate with both traditional and non-traditional players in the space of public health. The next chapter, therefore, looks at how the World Bank can cooperate with countries, institutions and corporates in building effective and efficient global health systems.

Chapter 6

World Bank Partnership and the Global Pandemic Playbook

The World Bank is a critical player within the global health architecture. For the Pandemic Playbook to be enacted, the World Bank needs to be the leading partner. This chapter outlines how to make that happen. In brief, The Bank Group will remain a trusted partner with its current collaborators, and must also become an innovative connector with other new and current actors in order to make the global public health system effective and resilient. This chapter identifies some of the areas where the World Bank could contribute to strengthening the global health systems by cooperating with other agencies. It will then highlight how this unified partnership can address and coordinate the elements of the Global Pandemic Playbook. The components of this Global Pandemic Playbook will include ways to globally coordinate the following responses to the next wave of pandemic diseases:

- Foresight, Anticipation & Early Warning Systems
- Planning & Mobilization
- Collective Intelligence & Innovation
- Prevention and Basic Health Infrastructure
- Regulatory & Standards Framework
- Mitigation and Stimulus

As we will see in this chapter, the past and present work of the World Bank and the actions that other actors have taken to strengthen global public health can be unified to respond with clarity and coordination to the next global pandemic that comes our way.

Here are the areas for partnership:

Foresight, Anticipation and Early Warning Systems

There is a need for the World Bank to work closely with the United Nations systems and countries to forge a common understanding of global health security. Scientific evidence is clear that infectious diseases will be commonplace in the future, and the main sources of this wave of disease are climate change and viruses. However, the global community was caught unprepared for the current pandemic because there is a lack of common understanding of health security, and, unfortunately, health cooperation was not effective. To this end, it is important for the World Bank, in partnership with other actors, to overcome the cycle of neglect and panic by ensuring that countries and institutions understand what is at stake when it comes to global health security. This will only be possible when individual nations, as well as the international community, act on the urgent understanding of the shared fate, mutual obligations, and greater solidarity necessary in the twenty-first century. This is the only feasible way to save humanity from the existential threats posed by thousands of pathogens surrounding us.

The current pandemic has underscored the importance of coordinated monitoring, warning and joint responses to global health threats. By so doing, the World Bank will contribute to improving and scaling up monitoring and information sharing at a global scale and thereby foster closer international coordination. Meanwhile, a health emergency joint-action program should be established for global health emergencies, under which national contingents of first responders can conduct joint simulation exercises regularly to evaluate national, regional, and global preparedness and response capabilities. To improve the efficiency of such a program, related deployment and authorization mechanisms need to be introduced so that multilateral assistance will be readily available when cross-border and global health crises occur.

Planning and Mobilization

We have learned in the previous chapter that the ultimate responsibility for health outcome lies with national governments through their reforms and investments in the health sector. However, financing the health sector has always been challenging in low and middle-income countries. There are two explanations for this. First, the budget of the ministry of health has, in most countries, relied on donor funding, which tends to be very unpredictable. Second, investments in this sector are not appealing in the eyes of politicians who are only looking for quick wins to show to their electorates. Improving public health systems is a long-term project, where the success will be played out in future pandemics and crises. Short-term wins are fewer – and these are what typically appeal most to governments. That said, there is a need for the World Bank to help its client countries improve financing mechanisms for global public health by clearly articulating that public health is a national security issue, and that increasing investment in national public health is good for the economy. This work aligns squarely with the Bank's efforts to help client countries increase resource mobilization and spending efficiency by investing wisely.

Relatedly, most, if not all, low- and middle-income countries have disaster management units, which tend to be less effective in the event of a disaster due to lack of resources. It is time that these units are well resourced and to find a mechanism by which earmarked disaster resources would be able to be used flexibly in the event no disaster occurs. Most importantly, countries should now expand the scope of these units to include not only natural disasters, such as floods or earthquakes, but also health emergencies. Past occurrences clearly show that natural disasters tend to be followed by health disasters.

Last but not least, and as proposed in the previous chapter, the

World Bank should leverage the plethora of actors in the space of public health to maximize resources needed to finance health investments and necessary reforms. These actors, who are new and unusual partners for the World Bank include: nation states' agencies, multilateral private corporations, philanthropies, and the civil society.

As each of these are already playing a part in the response globally to pandemic disease, the World Bank can organize involvement with them around its Human Capital Initiative. The results of this initiative necessitate the involvement of complex and coordinated actors. In light of the COVID-19 pandemic, we can see how intertwined all aspects of human capital are with disease interception, prevention, and response. We need to plan for on-the-ground implementation that would help nations focus their attention to the recurrent issue of global pandemics.

Collective Intelligence and Innovations

We have all learned how contact tracing apps are useful during the COVID-19 outbreak, and how the Chinese system developed after SARS, if used effectively, could have served as an early warning system. The Bank should collaborate with other actors in the health space to fund the development and scaleup of those innovations so that they can easily be tweaked and used in the future whenever humanity is exposed to similar situations. The Bank should explore how the Chinese Alert System could be scaled up and installed in most zoonosis hotspots where outbreaks of disease are highly likely. Innovations of this type could help with early preparedness and limit the spread of outbreaks. The Bank should also work with other actors to help countries create a conducive environment to nurture health-related innovations such as vaccines and medications to treat disease, as well as innovations that will include health and disease responses. By supporting regulatory reforms and initial investments, the World Bank can encourage both innovation and the creation of necessary firewalls to protect the privacy of the population without compromising the privacy of data providers, nor violating medical ethics.

The response to the current pandemic in terms of vaccine development has been impressive. At the time of writing, about 170 vaccines were in development. However, as detailed above, because the global health system is fragmented, this effort is too broad and too uncoordinated. With a global response, the World Bank could coordinate the use of funds, pooling and sharing resources to develop few, but promising, vaccines, without duplication of effort or redundancies.

Additionally, there is an urgent need for new arrangements at the global level to facilitate the development, finance, production and equitable distribution of COVID-19 vaccines. While the Coalition for Epidemic Preparedness Innovations is working on financing and developing vaccines, it has left out a large group of developing countries that urgently need the equitable distribution of those vaccines. Although the Bank Group is part of the Coalition, there is no guarantee that the Bank can ensure equitable distribution to low-and middle-income countries with the current structure. In order to have a robust response to future pandemics, the Bank needs to stand as a coordinator of these efforts along with other agencies, and to address the inequities we have witnessed in the COVID-19 response.

Prevention and Basic Health Infrastructure

The global supply chains and distribution networks, particularly of medical equipment and supplies, have never been subjected to harsher conditions than during the global peak of COVID-19. While these supply and distribution chains served the world sufficiently in more ideal situations, during the COVID-19 pandemic, countries had to scramble to get necessary medical supplies and equipment, because they were in short supply, and their transportation was challenging due to reduced number of flights and ships as well as a freeze in production due to pandemic-containment measures.

It is crucial to create a worldwide basic health care infrastructure. This means that we need a global system that understands the harsh reality that if there is insufficient health infrastructure in one country, contagion becomes an issue for all countries, as fast as a plane can fly. The World Bank has a history of providing health infrastructure services and has expertise in coordinating this complex field. It should be at the top of the priorities of what the new global pandemic preparedness entity would be tasked to do. Sufficient health infrastructure outside of pandemics would go a long way in the prevention, preparedness, containment, and response to any future pandemic.

What is clear from the disruption in the supply chains of medical supplies and equipment is that countries should optimize their public health resource reserves and allocation systems to build a worldwide medical product stockpile and resilient supply chains. Public health resources should be increased to create a global strategic stockpile. At the same time, the world also needs reliable and resilient global medical product supply chains. These should be coupled with sound logistics and management to ensure the worldwide availability of urgently needed medical materials in the event of a health crisis.

International scientific collaboration should be increased to facilitate technological innovation in drug resistance research. Countries should establish a public health technology bank to ensure the reliable supply of diagnostic kits, vaccines, and treatments. The World Bank Group, through its International Finance Corporation (IFC) network of clients, could help countries navigate this challenge before the next pandemic hits. This can be done by encouraging the establishment of a regional stockpile for essential medical supplies that can be readily deployed for emergency needs. What is crucial, though, is the preservation of open markets for trade and investments, which ensures the resilience of supply chains for essential goods such as food, medicines, medical supplies, and other essential products.

Regulatory and Standards Frameworks

We have noted in the previous chapters that the world could have been saved from the pandemic if the country of origin was able to share information on the outbreak on time. However, this happened in the presence of WHO's International Health Regulations, which obligates every nation to share information on the outbreak or unknown health issue. But, as it turned out, even that sharing is at the discretion of the respective country and even at the discretion of local health authorities who can withhold vital information from the government. To this end, it is clear that the International Health Regulations need to be reformed to reflect the current landscape of global health, and enforcement mechanisms. National governments should be supported to honor their commitments by increasing health investments and personnel training, improving interagency coordination, establishing new health partnerships, and enhancing health emergency preparedness. All these initiatives should help developing countries upgrade their health information systems with a view of automating information flows across nations as well as becoming guardians of global public health. The World Bank should work closely with the World Health Organization, which is legally entrusted with developing regulations and standards for health procedures and processes by increasing financial and technical assistance to developing countries to be able to build a robust global public health system.

Mitigation and Stimulus

The next disaster is a matter of "when," not "if." In this regard, there is a need for internationally coordinated efforts to mitigate not only pandemics, but other possible disasters – such as those caused by climate change. The urgency of addressing these issues should be clearly articulated to the general public to forge a common understanding of what is at stake when it comes to their health security. The world's future will depend on how nations cooperate globally, synchronize efforts, and maximize their combined potential.

Disaster education programs are increasingly essential as the frequency of occurrences increases. In this regard, the World Bank should work with client countries to strengthen their disaster education programs as these programs are critical in preventing panic or complacency in the event of a disaster. These programs should start educating citizens at an early age to inform them how to respond and act during disasters. Society should be kept abreast of preparations and ready to deal with any calamity. Proper education in hygiene and personal behavior, as well as common sense, will be crucial for humanity's survival. Knowledge on these issues should be encouraged and given their due respect. In light of COVID-19 and the experiences of the global community, it is imperative that education programs on disasters are prioritized and put front and center. It is through knowledge, training, and awareness that we will be able to move global actors and citizens to follow the path that has been created by the scientific community. We are talking about compliance with simple behaviors like wearing masks and social distancing, which seem simple from a scientific angle but need education to gain compliance. From a young age, children should be educated about pandemics in the same way they are educated about other issues in the environment that require knowledge and training, such as malaria prevention.

We have learned during the current crisis that some

pandemic-containment measures have been less effective in containing the spread of outbreaks simply because of people's need for economic livelihood. People in developing countries were severely affected because many of them work in the informal economy, and social safety nets do not cover them. The World Bank, in partnership with governments and institutions, needs to devise social safety nets that cover many people in developing countries, and are fiscally sustainable. These safety nets will be crucial to the success of any pandemic response and will ensure compliance with health regulations and a sense of stability for the world's most vulnerable populations without whom no pandemic plan is complete.

Conclusion

This section looked at how the World Bank can cooperate with other stakeholders in the space of global health to make the global health system effectively respond to pandemics. The main areas of collaboration are, to a large extent, determined by the Bank Group's comparative advantages. On this basis, six areas of engagements have been identified: foresight, anticipation and early warning systems; planning and mobilization; collective intelligence and innovation; prevention and basic health infrastructure; regulatory and standards frameworks and mitigation and stimulus.

My conviction that the World Bank is the correct entity to coordinate the Global Pandemic Playbook response to the next pandemic comes from the World Bank's history of responding to the outcries of needs. In my capacity as a member of the Executive Board, I have heard these outcries, and I know the Bank places high value on meeting those needs. The Bank has created an environment where it can be flexible, innovative, and comprehensive. With the addition of the ability to work with new partners across the globe, I have the immense hope that this proposal will seriously impact the success of our global response to future pandemics.

This is not a proposal for the next few years as we recover from COVID-19. It is a proposal for long-term planning for the inevitable future pandemics. We should have a world where pandemics do not catch us by surprise. Through proper pandemic and crises planning, we can create solid health care systems across the globe. We can mobilize in the face of early warning signals. We can respond with coordination and unity, including our combined economic and regulatory actions. Such a global response could come quickly, with little duplication of efforts, and with evenness across the globe, erasing the inequities we have seen in the past. Working together from one global playbook, we could greatly reduce the devastation and loss we have historically suffered from pandemic diseases.

Chapter 7

Epilogue

A historical account of pandemics, along with the current pandemic's evolving story, has revealed the critical importance of global public health to the proper functioning of the global economy, and thereby to the world's development at large. We have all witnessed how our global systems, starting from supply chains to the political leadership to health systems, have been put to unprecedented tests among all countries and across the income spectrum during the COVID-19 pandemic. The global response to the pandemic has been fragmented, reflecting the underlying shortcomings of the global systems which existed well before the pandemic.

One manifestation of the flaws of our global systems was the failure to listen to science, particularly medical science, despite its enormous contribution to post-World War II prosperity and civilization. Consequently, the pandemic caught the world unprepared, despite repeated warnings that humanity has been increasingly exposed to existential threats from millions of pathogens. Worse, due to climate change, humankind's vulnerability and fragility are ever-increasing.

The pandemic's impacts, including loss of lives and contraction of economies, point to the urgent need for building resilient global systems if we are to futureproof our development while safeguarding the development gains which we have been able to achieve over the last decades. This pandemic has taught us that, absent strongly coordinated global efforts, decades of development could be wiped out in less than one year. The question then is how countries could regroup and systematically build the resilience required to protect one another against the devastating impact of the next pandemic, which, according to epidemiological models and history of pandemics, is a matter of a few years, not decades, to come. Part of the answer to this question lies in reforming the very institutions the international community has entrusted with the responsibilities of looking after our shared areas of interests, ranging from trade to health and development. In this particular case, the World Bank Group is a key actor whose reforms, if unanimously supported, could be a post-pandemic world game-changer. Compared to other actors in the global economic landscape, the World Bank Group is uniquely placed to lead the international community to a safe new world due to its long history in the realm of development, starting with the recovery of Europe in the aftermath of World War II to supporting the transition of Eastern European and Asian economies from centrally planned to market economies. Above all, the ongoing pandemic gives the Bank an edge over comparable institutions because any recovery effort and subsequent resilience-building have to be coordinated under the health-development nexus, a natural extension of the World Bank's mission of eradicating poverty and boosting shared prosperity. More precisely, the nexus aligns well with the Bank's renewed focus on how underinvestment in human capital translated to suboptimal economic development in low- and lower-middle-income countries. For the future safety and prosperity of our world, this investment in human capital on all levels from education to economics to health care needs to be strong and well organized.

Despite the World Bank's comparative advantages in leading the international community towards the pandemic-resilient world, it is crucial to leverage synergies with other key actors with more specialized mandates. It is the coming together of all key players in the realm of global health governance and global economic governance that will be a deciding factor, if we hope to respond better to the next pandemic. To have any positive outcome, we must be able to put in place a resilient global public health framework and address underlying vulnerabilities inherent in the current global health and economic systems. We should and must envision a global system in which countries at various levels of development come together in an environment of equity to chart a common course against any global public crisis or emergency threatening our lives and livelihoods.

Education and health systems are primary channels through which resilience against pandemics is built. However, the COVID-19 pandemic has clearly demonstrated that these systems failed to serve that purpose. The global community is, therefore, in need of education and health systems that prepare people for pandemics by first acknowledging the importance of pandemic-containment measures in saving their lives. Education is also critical to ensuring that political leadership listens to scientific guidance. To be successful, national curricula at all levels of education should mainstream disaster management to inculcate the skills required to respond to pandemic or disasters and appreciate the magnitude of the impact caused by pandemics. More importantly, people should have equitable access to quality health services, essentially a basic right of every citizen. This will be possible only when sufficient investments are made in all facets of the health sector based on each country's needs assessment, an exercise that every nation should conduct during or immediately after the current pandemic. Countries can promote and ensure equity in accessing health services by identifying and acquiring access to reliable supplies of medical supplies and equipment, building enough medical facilities and training an adequate number of medical personnel to serve current and future populations. These medium- and long-term investments require proper planning, and for developing countries, an international support, as well as appreciation from the political leadership of the need to consider these as complementary investments needed to spur economic development.

The COVID-19 pandemic has disproportionately hit low- and middle-income countries. These are the countries where pandemic responses have been fairly limited and have depended on international support. This paradox largely reflects where our current system has fallen short. We need a global system that will protect the most vulnerable and build the resilience of economies in the wake of future pandemics. The envisioned solid and resilient global system will ensure that pandemic-containment measures do not weigh heavily on the people working in the informal sector by ensuring that they have adequate social safety nets. While establishing near-universal social safety nets is an ideal strategy to protect marginalized people in the event of shocks, there is also an urgent need to ensure that countries are economically better prepared. This preparedness entails a host of interventions that respective countries, along with the international community, will need to carry out over the medium to long term. Available evidence suggests that underlying vulnerabilities inherent in most developing countries have increased the pandemic's impact. Some of the factors which limited developing countries' responses to the pandemic include high debt levels, a high percentage of the work force in the informal economy, heavy dependence on a few primary commodities and weak health systems. Tackling these structural constraints has many benefits to developing countries, including improving the country's ability to respond to the pandemic. The World Bank is best placed, along with other key actors, to support and implement a jobs and economic transformation agenda, as a key component of building economic resilience.

The prosperity we all strive to safeguard today in the wake of the COVID-19 pandemic was made possible through countries' engagements in travel, trade, and investment. We, therefore, need to build a global system that will deepen, not weaken, coordination and collaboration among a multitude of actors from various sectors in a bid to improve the well-being of the global community. This is possible only if we all acknowledge that a fenced-off world makes us poorer and more exposed to pandemic diseases due to diminished cooperation and limited information sharing. If we close our borders to aid and assistance, creating what we think of as independence, that does not mean the next pandemic will do the same. In an interconnected world, infectious diseases easily transcend borders and have far-reaching impacts across countries, and, worse, across generations.

This contagion will further be compounded by climate change that also respects no border. Undoubtedly, we are living in a world where most scientific evidence points to catastrophes of a global scale which no one country, rich or poor, could handle alone. Our interconnectedness implies that a pandemic anywhere is a pandemic everywhere. The COVID-19 pandemic has painfully taught us just that. In the event of a global public catastrophe, the first and most important line of defense is our global cooperation. Thus, shortcomings in international cooperation highlighted by the current pandemic should serve as entry points to further deepen our commitments to our shared prosperity, including building pandemic-resilient global health and economic systems.

COVID-19 has surpassed most modern pandemics in morbidity and mortality and triggered a crisis of immense and enormous proportionality. While the world has moved swiftly to contain a further outbreak of the coronavirus and poured billions of dollars to prevent economic fallout, a third crisis is about to hit. That third crisis will be a food crisis that is not due to shortage but as the result of disruption of global food supply and distribution chains precipitated by the pandemic.

We are learning that we can't afford to respond to the current pandemic exclusively as a health problem without seeing it as a development challenge too, and that multifaced interventions are required. The international community has learned much but acted on little from recent pandemics; we simply cannot be complacent after the current pandemic is over. The global community must learn, and learn quickly, that we need to build resilient health and economic systems to minimize avoidable loss of life and unnecessary disruption of economies. A pandemic-resilient world is possible. But it will not happen on its own, and it will take time to build. If we all agree that the pandemic before us is a development challenge addressing all aspects of life across all the world, it is incumbent upon the World Bank to take a leadership role in coordinating efforts required to institute pandemic-resilient global health and economic systems that deliver inclusive economic growth, prosperity and safety for all.

Endnotes

1   "1918 Pandemic Influenza Historic Timeline | Pandemic Influenza (Flu) | CDC," April 18, 2019, https://www.cdc.gov/flu/pandemic-resources/1918-commemoration/pandemic-timeline-1918.htm.

2   Ibid.

3   Crosby, A.W. (2003). America's Forgotten Pandemic: The Influenza of 1918. 2end ed. Cambridge: Cambridge University Press.

4   Fenner, Frank, Henderson, Donald A, Arita, Isao, Jezek, Zdenek, Ladnyi, Ivan Danilovich. et al. (1988). Smallpox and its eradication / F. Fenner ... [et al.]. World Health Organization. https://www.who.int/bulletin/volumes/86/12/08-041208/en/

5   "Global HIV & AIDS Statistics — 2020 Fact Sheet," accessed September 2, 2020, https://www.unaids.org/en/resources/fact-sheet. Content Source: HIV govDate last updated: July 07 and 2020, "Global HIV/AIDS Overview," HIV.gov, July 7, 2020, https://www.hiv.gov/federal-response/pepfar-global-aids/global-hiv-aids-overview.

6   "WHO | Chapter 1: Global Health: Today's Challenges," WHO (World Health Organization), accessed September 2, 2020, https://www.who.int/whr/2003/chapter1/en/index3.html.

7   "Basic Statistics | HIV Basics | HIV/AIDS | CDC," July 1, 2020, https://www.cdc.gov/hiv/basics/statistics.html.

8   "SARS | Frequently Asked Questions | CDC," February 8, 2019, https://www.cdc.gov/sars/about/faq.html.

9   ibid

10 "Severe Acute Respiratory Syndrome (SARS)," accessed September 2, 2020, https://www.who.int/westernpacific/health-topics/severe-acute-respiratory-syndrome.

11 Severe Acute Respiratory Syndrome (SARS) Epidemiology and Working Group, "Consensus Document on the Epidemiology of Severe Acute Respiratory Syndrome (SARS)" (World Health Organization Department of Communicable Disease Surveillance and Response, May 2003), https://www.who.int/csr/sars/en/WHOconsensus.pdf?ua=1.

12 "Severe Acute Respiratory Syndrome (SARS)," accessed September 2, 2020, https://www.who.int/westernpacific/health-topics/severe-acute-respiratory-syndrome.

13 "SARS | Basics Factsheet | CDC," February 8, 2019, https://www.cdc.gov/sars/about/fs-sars.html.

14 CDC, "2009 H1N1 Pandemic," Centers for Disease Control and Prevention, June 11, 2019, https://www.cdc.gov/flu/pandemic-resources/2009-h1n1-pandemic.html.

15 Ibid.

16 CDC, "2009 H1N1 Pandemic," Centers for Disease Control and Prevention, June 11, 2019, https://www.cdc.gov/flu/pandemic-resources/2009-h1n1-pandemic.html.

17 "Coronavirus Disease (COVID-19)," accessed September 3, 2020, https://www.who.int/emergencies/diseases/novel-coronavirus-2019.

18 "Italy Announces Restrictions Over Entire Country in Attempt to Halt Coronavirus – The New York Times," accessed September 3, 2020, https://www.nytimes.com/2020/03/09/world/europe/italy-lockdown-coronavirus.html.

19 "COVID-19 to Plunge Global Economy into Worst Recession since World War II," World Bank, accessed September 3, 2020, https://www.worldbank.org/en/news/press-release/2020/06/08/covid-19-to-plunge-global-economy-into-worst-recession-since-world-war-ii.

20 Ibid.

21 "World Bank Predicts Sharpest Decline of Remittances in Recent History," Text/HTML, World Bank, accessed

September 2, 2020, https://www.worldbank.org/en/news/press-release/2020/04/22/world-bank-predicts-sharpest-decline-of-remittances-in-recent-history.

22 Walker, P.G.T et al (202). The Impact of COVID-19 and Strategies for Mitigation and Suppression in Low- and Middle-Income Countries. Science 365 (6502):413-422. Retrieved from https://science.sciencemag.org/content/369/6502/413/tab-pdf

23 "Who We Are," accessed September 2, 2020, https://www.who.int/about/who-we-are.

24 Ibid.

25 "World Bank Group: 100 Countries Get Support in Response to COVID-19 (Coronavirus)," World Bank, accessed September 2, 2020, https://www.worldbank.org/en/news/press-release/2020/05/19/world-bank-group-100-countries-get-support-in-response-to-covid-19-coronavirus.

26 "IDB Group Announces Priority Support Areas for Countries Affected by COVID-19 I IADB," accessed September 2, 2020, https://www.iadb.org/en/news/idb-group-announces-priority-support-areas-countries-affected-covid-19.

27 Asian Development Bank, "ADB's COVID-19 Response Reaches $9.3 Billion to End-July 2020," Text, Asian Development Bank (Asian Development Bank, August 3, 2020), https://www.adb.org/news/adbs-covid-19-response-reaches-93-billion-end-july-2020.

28 "The EBRD's Coronavirus Solidarity Package," accessed September 2, 2020, //www.ebrd.com/what-we-do/coronavirus-solidarity.

29 "Jack Ma Foundation Donates Masks, Testing Kits to Africa for COVID-19 Control - Xinhua I English.News.Cn," accessed September 2, 2020, http://www.xinhuanet.com/english/2020-03/17/c_138887624.htm. http://www.xinhuanet.com/english/2020-03/17/c_138887624.htm

30 "Gates Foundation Expands Commitment to COVID-19

Response, Calls for International Collaboration," January 1, 1AD, https://www.gatesfoundation.org/ Media-Center/Press-Releases/2020/04/Gates-Foundation-Expands-Commitment-to-COVID-19-Response-Calls-for-International-Collaboration.

31 This amount is equivalent to 11 percent of the US GDP.

32 "Policy Responses to COVID19," accessed September 2, 2020, https://www.imf.org/en/Topics/imf-and-covid19/Poli cy-Responses-to-COVID-19#U.

33 "COVID-19 Contributions Tracker," accessed September 2, 2020, https://www.who.int/emergencies/diseases/novel-coronavirus-2019/donors-and-partners/funding.

34 "How Much Are African Countries Spending to Help the Poorest Deal with COVID19? – Development Reimagined," accessed September 2, 2020, https:// developmentreimagined.com/2020/04/27/how-much-are-african-countries-spending/.

35 "Policy Brief: Education during COVID-19 and Beyond" (New York, NY: The United Nations, n.d.), https://www. un.org/sites/un2.un.org/files/sg_policy_brief_covid-19_ and_education_august_2020.pdf.

36 Ibid.

37 "Melinda Gates: COVID-19's Toll on Women," Foreign Affairs. accessed September 3, 2020, https://www. foreignaffairs.com/articles/world/2020-07-15/melinda-gates-pandemics-toll-women.

38 "COVID-19 and the World of Work: Updated Estimates and Analysis," vol. Third Edition (International Labour Organization, 2020), https://www.ilo.org/wcmsp5/groups/ public/---dgreports/---dcomm/documents/briefingnote/ wcms_743146.pdf.

39 Elizabeth Cameron, Jennifer Nuzzo, and Jessica Bell, "Global Health Security Index" (Johns Hopkins Center for Health Security, October 2019).

40 Deborah Mackenzie, *COVID-19: The Pandemic That Never Should Have Happened, and How to Stop the Next One* (New Yorkm NY: Hachett Book Group, 2020).

41 Ibid.

42 Ibid.

43 "Local Officials in China Hid Coronavirus Dangers From Beijing, U.S. Agencies Find – The New York Times," accessed September 2, 2020, https://www.nytimes.com/2020/08/19/world/asia/china-coronavirus-beijing-trump.html

44 Gates, B. "Responding to Covid-19 - A Once-in-a Century Pandemic?" (*The New England Journal of Medicine, 2020), 382*(18), 1677-1679.

45 "The Human Capital Project," The World Bank (2018). accessed September 2, 2020, https://www.worldbank.org/en/publication/human-capital.

46 Ibid.

About the Author

Anne Kabagambe served as an Executive Director at the World Bank Group from 2016 to 2020. She was responsible for a constituency of 22 African nations as well as fiduciary responsibilities as a member of the Budget Committee, the Committee on Development Effectiveness, the Pension Benefits Committee, and co-chaired the Board's Gender Working Group. Anne has over 35 years of work experience in the development field. She is a citizen of Uganda.

CHANGEMAKERS
BOOKS

TRANSFORMATION

Transform your life, transform your world – Changemakers
Books publishes for individuals committed to transforming
their lives and transforming the world. Our readers seek
to become
positive, powerful agents of change. Changemakers Books
inform, inspire, and provide practical wisdom and skills to
empower us to write the next chapter of humanity's future.
www.changemakers-books.com

The *Resilience* Series

The Resilience Series is a collaborative effort by the authors of Changemakers Books in response to the 2020 coronavirus epidemic. Each concise volume offers expert advice and practical exercises for mastering specific skills and abilities. Our intention is that by strengthening your resilience, you can better survive and even thrive in a time of crisis.
www.resilience-books.com

Adapt and Plan for the New Abnormal - in the COVID-19 Coronavirus Pandemic
Gleb Tsipursky

Aging with Vision, Hope and Courage in a Time of Crisis
John C. Robinson

Connecting With Nature in a Time of Crisis
Melanie Choukas-Bradley

Going Within in a Time of Crisis
P. T. Mistlberger

Grow Stronger in a Time of Crisis
Linda Ferguson

Handling Anxiety in a Time of Crisis
George Hoffman

Navigating Loss in a Time of Crisis
Jules De Vitto

The Life-Saving Skill of Story
Michelle Auerbach

**Virtual Teams - Holding the Center When You Can't
Meet Face-to-Face**
Carlos Valdes-Dapena

Virtually Speaking - Communicating at a Distance
Tim Ward and Teresa Erickson

Current Bestsellers from Changemakers Books

Pro Truth
A Practical Plan for Putting Truth Back into Politics
Gleb Tsipursky and Tim Ward

How can we turn back the tide of post-truth politics, fake news, and misinformation that is damaging our democracy? In the lead up to the 2020 US Presidential Election, Pro Truth provides the answers.

An Antidote to Violence
Evaluating the Evidence
Barry Spivack and Patricia Anne Saunders

It's widely accepted that Transcendental Meditation can create peace for the individual, but can it create peace in society as a whole? And if it can, what could possibly be the mechanism?

Finding Solace at Theodore Roosevelt Island
Melanie Choukas-Bradley

A woman seeks solace on an urban island paradise in Washington D.C. through 2016-17, and the shock of the Trump election.

the bottom
a theopoetic of the streets
Charles Lattimore Howard

An exploration of homelessness fusing theology, jazz-verse and intimate storytelling into a challenging, raw and beautiful tale.

The Soul of Activism
A Spirituality for Social Change
Shmuly Yanklowitz

A unique examination of the power of interfaith spirituality to
fuel the fires of progressive activism.

Future Consciousness
The Path to Purposeful Evolution
Thomas Lombardo

An empowering evolutionary vision of wisdom and the human
mind to guide us in creating a positive future.

Preparing for a World that Doesn't Exist - Yet
Rick Smyre and Neil Richardson

This book is about an emerging Second Enlightenment and the
capacities you will need to achieve success in this new, fast-
evolving world.